THEORY
OF ACTION

Lawrence H. Davis

UNIVERSITY OF MISSOURI-ST. LOUIS

PRENTICE-HALL, INC.
Englewood Cliffs, New Jersey *07632*

Library of Congress Cataloging in Publication Data

Davis, Lawrence Howard, date
  Theory of action.

  (Prentice-Hall foundations of philosophy series)
  Bibliography: p.
  Includes index.
  1. Act (Philosophy) 2. Events (Philosophy)
3. Free will and determinism. I. Title.
B105.A35D38   123   78-9542
ISBN 0-13-913152-3
ISBN 0-13-913145-0 pbk.

In gratitude to the Agent
whose activity is with us continually,
and upon whose will all human agency depends

תושלב"ע

© *1979*
by PRENTICE-HALL, INC.
Englewood Cliffs, New Jersey 07632

10 9 8 7 6 5 4 3 2 1

PRENTICE-HALL INTERNATIONAL, INC., *London*
PRENTICE-HALL OF AUSTRALIA PTY. LIMITED, *Sydney*
PRENTICE-HALL OF CANADA, LTD., *Toronto*
PRENTICE-HALL OF INDIA PRIVATE LIMITED, *New Delhi*
PRENTICE-HALL OF JAPAN, INC., *Tokyo*
PRENTICE-HALL OF SOUTHEAST ASIA PTE. LTD., *Singapore*
WHITEHALL BOOKS LIMITED, *Wellington, New Zealand*

PRENTICE-HALL FOUNDATIONS OF PHILOSOPHY SERIES

Virgil Aldrich	Philosophy of Art
William Alston	Philosophy of Language
Roderick M. Chisholm	Theory of Knowledge
Lawrence H. Davis	Theory of Action
William Dray	Philosophy of History
Joel Feinberg	Social Philosophy
William K. Frankena	Ethics
Martin P. Golding	Philosophy of Law
Carl Hempel	Philosophy of Natural Science
John H. Hick	Philosophy of Religion
David L. Hull	Philosophy of Biological Science
James E. McClellan	Philosophy of Education
Willard Van Orman Quine	Philosophy of Logic
Richard Rudner	Philosophy of Social Science
Wesley C. Salmon	Logic
Jerome Shaffer	Philosophy of Mind
Richard Taylor	Metaphysics

Elizabeth and Monroe Beardsley, editors

FOUNDATIONS OF PHILOSOPHY

Many of the problems of philosophy are of such broad relevance to human concerns, and so complex in their ramifications, that they are, in one form or another, perennially present. Though in the course of time they yield in part to philosophical inquiry, they may need to be rethought by each age in the light of its broader scientific knowledge and deepened ethical and religious experience. Better solutions are found by more refined and rigorous methods. Thus, one who approaches the study of philosophy in the hope of understanding the best of what it affords will look for both fundamental issues and contemporary achievements.

Written by a group of distinguished philosophers, the Foundations of Philosophy Series aims to exhibit some of the main problems in the various fields of philosophy as they stand at the present stage of philosophical history.

While certain fields are likely to be represented in most introductory courses in philosophy, college classes differ widely in emphasis, in method of instruction, and in rate of progress. Every instructor needs freedom to change his course as his own philosophical interests, the size and makeup of his classes, and the needs of his students vary from year to year. The seventeen volumes in the Foundations of Philosophy Series—each complete in itself, but complementing the others—offer a new flexibility to the instructor, who can create his own textbook by combining several volumes as he wishes, and can choose different combinations at different times. Those volumes that are not used in an introductory course will be found valuable, along with other texts or collections of readings, for the more specialized upper-level courses.

Elizabeth Beardsley / *Monroe Beardsley*

CONTENTS

Contents

PREFACE

This book is intended as an introduction to contemporary philosophical discussions of human action. For each of the topics selected for chapter-length treatment, I have tried to present all the rival views which seem to be current as thoroughly and sympathetically as space and my own understanding have allowed. I also develop and defend my own position on each of the topics, subject to the same limitations, so this book presents *my* theory of action as well as a survey of the field known as "theory of action."

General readers with little or no previous exposure to contemporary philosophy may find the topics of the last chapters—the explanation of human actions, and free will—of greatest initial interest. But I believe these topics are best dealt with after one has achieved some clarity on what actions and related phenomena *are*. And I believe that puzzles and problems arising in the effort to do this are of great interest in themselves, as I have tried to indicate briefly in the Introduction and in the course of the chapters which follow. Perhaps the hottest topic in the field at present is one considered in Chapter 2, how actions are to be individuated, i.e., told apart, from one another. This may surprise the general reader. But I believe many will find (as I have) that one can get very caught up in the issue and the rival arguments long before coming to understand why (or if) it matters which position is correct.

The "action" in "theory of action" is limited to what single human beings do, and most of my examples are trivial: moving an arm, saying "Very good!" watering flowers, and the like. This procedure is typical of the field, and has its merits. When we agree about the explanation and freedom of trivial actions, we can then apply our results to actions of types arousing more emotion. And when we understand the nature of an individual's actions, we can ask if cooperative actions and actions of such "agents" as corporations, nations, and social classes are similar in any significant ways.

My effort to keep this book to a reasonable length has led to some concentration of arguments. For a general orientation, some readers may benefit from looking first at Jerome Shaffer's fine one-chapter treatment of the field in his *Philosophy of Mind,* in this same Prentice-Hall series.

The influence of my teachers Arthur C. Danto and Alvin I. Goldman will be evident to readers acquainted with their work, despite my frequent dissent from their views, and it is a pleasure to acknowledge my intellectual and personal debt to them. Special thanks are due to Hugh McCann for advice and constructive criticism at all stages of the research leading to this book, and to Robert Audi, who on very short notice supplied me with extensive comments on the penultimate draft. Many others gave similar aid on portions of the text and assorted precursors, including Michael Bratman, Robert C. Cummins, Dale Gottlieb, James W. Hall, Daniel L. Lehocky, and Ronald Munson. Collectively they saved me from many errors; I bear sole responsibility for those remaining. The editors of this series, Elizabeth and Monroe Beardsley, gave me helpful criticisms, welcome encouragement, and the very gentlest of prodding when my progress lagged.

I began thinking seriously about writing this book while on the faculty of the Johns Hopkins University, and did further research while a Visiting Fellow in the Humanities, Science, and Technology Unit of the Cornell University Program on Science, Technology, and Society, headed by Max Black. The book was completed with the help of a Summer Research Fellowship from the University of Missouri–St. Louis, where I now teach. I am indebted to Janiece Fister, Rita Larkin, and Kathleen Morris for typing the final drafts. Finally, I wish to record my gratitude to my wife, Sonya Meyers Davis, and my daughters Rena Freda and Miriam Shlomit, for bearing with me through the times when I neglected them in order to work on this book.

Lawrence H. Davis

Introduction

What is "free will"? Do we have it?

Theory of action is a relatively young branch of philosophy which has grown from attempts to clarify and answer these ancient questions. The answers are important. We value the freedom we think we have, and tend to think it confers a certain dignity on us and makes us into responsible beings. In the final chapter of this book, I will point toward what I think are the correct answers by defending an answer to a subsidiary question, whether our having "free will" is threatened by the doctrine of "determinism," the view that all we do happens by causal necessity.

But there are other questions, other problems.

In the last few centuries, there have emerged psychology and other sciences which deal with the behavior of human beings and other creatures. Historians have been writing for many more centuries, but it has never been clear whether they did so as scientists or as something else, perhaps humanists. It is often argued that even practitioners of the "human sciences" must be doing something very different than are their colleagues in physics and chemistry, since their subject matter—human action—is so different from what happens in the inanimate world. We will (in Chapter 5) address the specific question of whether human actions are *explained* in the same way that a physicist, say, might explain the collapse of a dam or the motion of a falling raindrop.

The first four chapters may be regarded simply as developing materials needed for discussing the topics of the last two chapters thoroughly and precisely. But the questions that will arise are of considerable interest in themselves. Some, like that of the difference between succeeding by "luck" and succeeding because one has the ability, are pretty much internal to theory of action. Others reflect broader issues in metaphysics, philosophy of mind, and ethics. "Abraham Lincoln died several days after being shot. When did the murder take place?"[1] "In accepting a job, I may know that I am preventing another applicant from taking it. Am I intentionally keeping him or her unemployed?" We will try to make clear on what the answers to questions like these depend.

The first main question before us is the one which really sparked the development of contemporary theory of action: what *are* actions? What are these things which manifest our hopefully free wills, are the chief interests of psychologists and historians, may be done intentionally or unwittingly, skillfully or by luck, and on some views may continue being done while their agents have gone elsewhere, as in the case of Lincoln's assassin? Or as Ludwig Wittgenstein phrased it, setting over two decades of philosophers busily to work:

Let us not forget this: when "I raise my arm," my arm goes up. And the problem arises: what is left over if I subtract the fact that my arm goes up from the fact that I raise my arm?[2]

For another person might have lifted my arm, or I might have suffered a nervous spasm. In neither case is my "free will" manifested, nor would what happens be explained in the ways allegedly special to human action. I have performed no action at all.

There is more to my raising my arm than my arm's rising. This statement refutes the view once popular among psychologists that actions are just "colorless movements," bare motions of parts of the agent's body. But recognizing the problem is no more than half of the solution, and students of the problem have not yet agreed on the remainder.

One promising way of inquiring further begins by noticing that agents have a *special awareness* of their actions which distinguishes these actions from mere motions of parts of their bodies. If someone lifts my arm, or it moves as the result of a nervous spasm, I will be aware that it is mov-

---

1 This example is discussed in John R. Silber, "Human Action and the Language of Volitions," *Proceedings of the Aristotelian Society*, LXIV (1964), 199–220.

2 Ludwig Wittgenstein, *Philosophical Investigations*, trans. G. E. M. Anscombe (New York: The Macmillan Company, 1953), sec. 621.

ing. But I will also be aware that *I* am not moving it. The "feeling"—this is perhaps not the right word for it—is entirely different when I move my arm and my doing so is an action. I am aware then that I am moving it, it is not simply moving.

This special awareness cannot itself be what must be added to the motion to get an action. Perhaps the missing ingredient is like the awareness, however, in being mental, or at least "inner" in some sense. In Chapter 1 we will look at more than one suggestion along these lines.

CHAPTER ONE

The Nature
of Action

ACTIONS, DOINGS, AND DOING-RELATED EVENTS

Moving my arm is something I do; my *doings* are to be contrasted with my *states,* things that I am. I may be frightened or excited, tall or fat, hungry, clumsy, watchful, tired, ill, or in good health. None of these are things that I do, and so none is my *action*. But what is the difference? In English and some other languages, doings are marked roughly by the possibility of using continuous tenses in the active voice. We can say "Sam is moving his arm," but we cannot say "Sam is being tall" except in special situations—for example, where Sam is a small boy pretending to be tall. But we can say "Sam is hoping for success" and "Sam is standing still," and here we seem to have states rather than doings. Since we are interested in actions, we can use the grammatical test as a definition of "doing," and concentrate on the question "What subclass of people's doings are their actions?" To regard hoping and standing still as things we "do" will then be harmless.

Even apart from things like hoping and standing still, actions are only a subclass of doings. People hiccup, bleed, tremble, shudder, stumble, and fall. They give birth, grow taller, fall asleep, catch cold, recuperate, faint, and die. Each of these is something people may be said to "do," yet none is an action. One person may observe another doing any of these things, and observing is itself a doing, but it is uncertain whether it is an action.

How can we distinguish actions from other doings?

One suggestion runs as follows. The bare motion of an arm is something the *arm* does; but when I move my arm, *I* do it. Actions would then be doings which we must say the *person* does, and not just some part of the body or even the whole body. Among the doings we have listed, this suggestion would eliminate bleeding, for example. Instead of saying "Sam is bleeding," we could as well and with greater accuracy say that his leg, or whatever, is bleeding. Similarly, we could say "Sam's body grew taller" instead of "Sam grew taller." But we cannot replace "Sam hiccupped" with "Sam's throat hiccupped" or anything similar, nor "Sam died" with "Sam's body died."[1] This seems to be more than a linguistic accident, though the reason for it is not clear. We must find a better suggestion.

When I move my arm, something happens—my arm moves—because I am moving it; we may say that I *make* it happen. A second suggestion, then, is that an action is a doing in which something happens—call it a *doing-related event*—because of what the person is doing. Perhaps this suggestion would show that stumbling, for example, is not an action. I do not "stumble because I am stumbling," I do not make my stumbling happen, and it is unclear what else could be the doing-related event. But this suggestion is still not adequate, since it would allow hiccupping to pass muster as an action: when I hiccup I make a sound, the sound occurs because I am hiccupping.

When I hiccup or stumble, what happens is not generally what I want to have happen, and much the same could be said for most of the other doings we mentioned which are not actions. What happens when a person gives birth may be exactly what was wanted, but it does not happen *because* the person wants it to, then and there. But when I move my arm, it seems the arm's motion occurs precisely because I want it to. This brings us to a third suggestion: an action is a doing in which a doing-related event occurs because the agent wants it to, then and there. Since desires are mental, this suggestion connects actions with their agents' minds, a connection whose plausibility we noted in the Introduction. Many regard this suggestion as entirely adequate, and we shall examine it more closely.

---

1 See Irving Thalberg, "Verbs, Deeds, and What Happens to Us," *Theoria*, 33 (1967), 259–77, or its revised version, "How Can We Distinguish between Doing and Undergoing?" in his *Enigmas of Agency* (New York: Humanities Press, Inc., 1972), pp. 48–72, for this point and others of interest.

DESIRE AND ACTION   To state the suggestion more precisely, we should first say more about doing-related events.

Every statement reporting an event represents that event as of a certain type. "There was a hiccupping sound" reports an event of the type "hiccupping-sound." "Sam's arm moved" reports one of the type "arm-motion." Doings are events. "Sam hiccupped" reports an event—a doing—of the type "hiccupping." "Sam moved his arm" reports one of the type "moving one's arm." Notice that "Sam hiccupped" implies "There was a hiccupping-sound," and "Sam moved his arm" implies "Sam's arm moved"; but in neither case does the converse implication hold. Sounds can be synthesized, and arms can be moved by external forces independent of the person to whom the arms are attached.

All the examples in this chapter will be like these. Corresponding to each type of doing A will be a type of event E_A such that "Someone did an A" (read "Someone did something of type A") implies "There was an E_A (i.e., an event of type E_A)," but "There was an E_A" does not imply "Someone did an A." (We will use capital letters for types of doings and other events. "A" is used rather than "D" because virtually all of our examples will be of types of action, *act-types,* rather than types of doings that are not actions. "Hiccupping" is an exception.)

We will conveniently assume that for each act-type A, we have identified the corresponding event-type E_A. But we should be aware that there is no automatic procedure for doing this. Perhaps "motion of one's legs adequate to propel one's body forward" corresponds to "walking forward." But why do we pick this rather than simply "forward motion of one's body"? We shall not try to say in general, except to note that often, "bringing about an E_A" or "making an E_A happen" will seem a plausible definition of the act-type A.

Suppose now that Sam has done an A. It follows that an E_A has occurred—often, it will be natural to say that Sam has brought about an E_A. This E_A that he has brought about is what we are calling a "doing-related event."

The suggestion we are examining may now be stated as the following two claims:[2]

(1) An agent's doing an A was an action only if an E_A occurred because the agent wanted one to, then and there.

(2) If an E_A occurred because an agent wanted one to, then and there, then the agent has done an A, and his doing so was an action.

---

[2] Sometimes the agent's doing an A is an action, and sometimes not. For example, not every doing of the type "bumping into the door" is an action. Each particular doing must be judged separately. Use of the past tense in (1) and (2) helps us remember this; the present tense might erroneously suggest that *every* time the agent does an A, it is an action.

The first says that for a case of action, it is *necessary* that a desire be present and play a certain role. The second says that for a case of action, it is *sufficient* that a desire be present and play this role.

Complications must and can be introduced into (1) to accommodate cases which would otherwise be counterexamples. Suppose Sam moved his arm because he wanted to frighten off a fly that had landed on it. Then (1) may seem to be false, because Sam's moving his arm was an action, though he did not "want" motion of his arm to occur; what he wanted was the departure of the fly, and motion of his arm was only a means to this end. In response, it is enough to explain that "wanting" is to be understood as including *wanting as means* as well as *wanting for its own sake.*

Other cases demand further explanations and even modifications of (1), and theorists have gone to great lengths to work them out.[3] Through all of them, the basic idea is preserved that in every case of action, something happens because the agent wants it to, then and there.[4] Unfortunately for this basic idea, the *necessity* of desire for action, there seem to be cases which no explanation or modification can accommodate, short of stretching the meaning of the word "wants" to a point where it has no useful content.

Consider the following examples:

(a) Sid visited his aunt because he thought he ought to do so.
(b) Sue stepped on the brake when a child suddenly darted out in the path of the car.
(c) Seth absent-mindedly brushed his teeth.
(d) Sal kicked the door in anger.
(e) Sol tore off the thread he had just noticed hanging from his shirt.

Sid might deny that he wanted to visit his aunt, and deny that he wanted to do any of the things he had to do as means to visiting her. Each step of the way to her door, he wished he were elsewhere. Only the recurring thought that he really ought to visit the woman kept him moving in her direction. Defenders of (1) and similar views usually claim that Sid must have "wanted to do his duty," and this desire was stronger than all his aversions to his aunt. But people sometimes do their duty just from a sense of duty. If this involves a desire, it must be admitted that it is a

---

[3] The most thorough effort along these lines is Alvin I. Goldman, *A Theory of Human Action* (Englewood Cliffs, N.J.: Prentice-Hall, Inc., 1970; Princeton Paperback, 1976). See also Donald Davidson, "Actions, Reasons, and Causes," *Journal of Philosophy*, LX (1963), 685–700, reprinted in Myles Brand, ed., *The Nature of Human Action* (Glenview, Ill.: Scott, Foresman and Company, 1970), pp. 67–79. See also the papers by Robert Audi cited in footnote 7, below. Goldman's book and Brand's anthology will be cited frequently in this and later chapters. We will use the abbreviations *"THA"* and *"NHA,"* respectively.

[4] This way of putting the basic idea, unlike (1) itself, allows for the possibility of unintentional actions, in which the agent does an A but had no desire for an E_A to occur. Instead, the agent wanted an event of some other type to occur.

desire of a very different kind from one, say, to eat lunch, or to frighten off a fly.

In (b), Sue might say after the fact that she "wanted" to stop the car. But need we take this literally? Why not say her foot moved against the pedal because she saw the child, and leave it at that? Certainly before she saw the child, she had no desire to stop. Did she suddenly experience a yearning, or an urge? Did she even have time for a thought of the desirability of stopping?[5] Or did she simply see the danger and respond instantly, like the good driver she is?

It is even less plausible to say a desire is present in (c). Seth may have gone to the medicine chest for an aspirin, but with his attention elsewhere, taken out the toothpaste and begun brushing from force of habit. Surely at no time in this interval did he judge it "desirable" to brush his teeth, nor did he find the thought "attractive." Rather, sight of the toothpaste, or his initial action of opening the medicine chest, triggered a routine pattern of activity.

In (d) it seems the doing-related event—the motion of Sal's foot against the door—occurred because of her anger, not because of any desire for it to happen. And in (e) we have action on impulse of a somewhat different sort. If asked why he tore off the thread, Sol might say, "No reason; I just did it." He might also say (as might Sal), "No reason; I just wanted to." But we should beware of taking such words as really indicating the presence of a desire because of which the doing-related event occurred. "I just wanted to" may simply be a conventional way of reinforcing the comment "No reason."

Perhaps there is a sense of the word "wants" in virtue of which (1) or some complicated version of it would not be falsified by these or other examples. But what definite content could it have? As a last resort, it may be suggested that in each case the person must have been "disposed" to do as he did, or "favorably inclined" toward the doing-related events which ensued.[6] One might as well say that a person whose knee is tapped by a doctor is disposed to jerk it, or favorably inclined toward its motion. Nothing remains of the conception of desire as a specific kind of mental phenomenon.[7]

---

[5] Goldman, *THA*, p. 94, implies that a mere thought of an action as "attractive" is all the "desire" required by his theory. Donald Davidson compares a desire to do something with a judgment that doing it would be "desirable" in "Intending," in Yirmiahu Yovel, ed., *Philosophy of History and Action* (Dordrecht: D. Reidel Publishing Company; Jerusalem: The Magnes Press, The Hebrew University, 1978).

[6] Goldman, *THA*, p. 49, and Jerome Shaffer, *Philosophy of Mind* (Englewood Cliffs, N.J.: Prentice-Hall, Inc., 1968), p. 84, suggest something like this.

[7] See Robert Audi, "Intending," *Journal of Philosophy*, LXX (1973), 387–403, and "The Concept of Wanting," *Philosophical Studies*, 24 (1973), 1–21, for another attempt to develop a concept of wanting which may be broad enough to shore up a version of (1).

We conclude that (1) is false in any illuminating sense, and that for action, it is *not necessary* that a desire play a certain role or even be present. What about (2)? If a desire is present, and does play the role indicated, is this *sufficient* for action?

It is generally agreed that the answer is "No." Imagine, for example, that a genuine mind reader is standing next to Sam, waiting to play the following trick on him. At the very moment Sam gets a desire for his arm to move, then and there, the mind reader reaches over and moves Sam's arm for him—before Sam himself can act on his desire. Here motion of the arm occurred because Sam wanted it to. The mind reader would not have moved it if Sam did not have this desire. Yet Sam did not *do* anything at all, except enter a certain state, a state of wanting motion of his arm. And he certainly did not act. By hypothesis, the mind reader beat him to it.

Examples like this show that for action it is not enough to have a doing-related event occur because of a desire. As Alvin Goldman has suggested, the desire and the event must be connected "in a certain characteristic way," a way not exemplified in the case of the mind reader. But what way is this? Goldman thinks we are

. . . aware, intuitively, of a characteristic manner in which desires and beliefs flow into intentional acts. Certainly we can "feel" a difference between a voluntary movement and an involuntary one, and this feeling . . . is symptomatic of certain causal processes.[8]

The route through the mind reader is ruled out, according to Goldman, just because it did not lead Sam to "feel" that the resulting motion of his arm was voluntary. He did not have his usual intuitive awareness that his desire for motion of his arm was in fact flowing into an intentional action.

If we take these remarks of Goldman seriously, we are brought finally to the "special awareness" that agents have of their actions as opposed to "mere" doing-related events, an awareness mentioned in the Introduction. Goldman is saying that besides a desire and a doing-related event, another feature X is necessary for action, and X is the feature which is the source of this special awareness.

But we have already argued that a desire is not necessary at all for action; and this raises another possibility. Perhaps feature X is by itself sufficient for action, as well as necessary—at least given the occurrence of an appropriate doing-related event. In the remainder of this chapter, we shall comment briefly on two theories which in effect develop this possibility, and then propose a third, which we will argue is most satisfactory.

8 From Alvin I. Goldman, *A Theory of Human Action* (copyright © 1970 by Alvin I. Goldman; Princeton Paperback, 1976), p. 62. Reprinted by permission of Princeton University Press. Goldman gives several other examples necessitating this conclusion.

Human agents have often been thought of as "active" in the sense that they can start chains of events in the world instead of only being links in chains already started. A billiard ball moves because struck by another; the motion of the first was communicated to it. But the first began moving because of the action of the player holding the cue stick; and the person was not simply transmitting an impetus received from elsewhere, but initiating the sequence of events which followed.

Some interpret this as incompatible with the kind of theory just presented. If Sam moved his arm, then the arm moved because of Sam and not because of a desire or anything else in Sam. Richard Taylor argues:

> If I believe that something not identical with myself was the cause of my behavior—some event wholly external to myself, for instance, or even one internal to myself, such as a nerve impulse, volition, or whatnot—then I cannot regard that behavior as being an act of mine, unless I further believe that I was the cause of that external or internal event.[9]

But we do not believe that we are (usually) the cause of our desires; nor, presumably, does Sam.

Usually when an inanimate object or even a person is said to "cause" something, what is meant is that some event involving the object or person caused it. We say the alarm clock awakened someone, and mean that *the alarm clock's ringing* caused him to wake up. We say Sam broke the vase, and mean that *his moving his arm* (so that it hit the vase) caused it to fall and break. But Taylor means something quite contrary to this.

In Taylor's view, alongside causation by events, we must recognize that there is such a thing as causation by agents. The vase's breaking was indeed caused by the motion of Sam's arm, and the motion of the arm was caused by muscular and neural events in Sam. But if "Sam broke the vase" reports an action, it must be the case on Taylor's view that one or more of those muscular and neural events was caused by Sam, directly, as we might put it. Direct causation of an event by an agent is a kind of phenomenon wholly unlike causation of an event by one or more others. It cannot be analyzed or explained in terms of causation by events, as we explained the alarm clock's awakening someone in terms of its *ringing* causing the person to wake up.

The *theory of agency*, then, is that every action involves direct causation of an event by an agent. "Some . . . causal chains . . . have beginnings," writes Taylor, "and they begin with agents themselves." In our terms:

[9] Richard Taylor, *Metaphysics*, 2nd ed. (Englewood Cliffs, N.J.: Prentice-Hall, Inc., 1974), p. 55; see also pp. 44–45 and 56–57. Taylor presents his position at length in his *Action and Purpose* (Englewood Cliffs, N.J.: Prentice-Hall, Inc., 1966). For criticism similar to that presented here, see Goldman, *THA*, pp. 80–85.

(3) An agent has done an A, and his doing so was an action, just in case an E_A occurred and was either itself directly caused by the agent, or caused by an event (or events) directly caused by the agent.

The main argument for this theory consists in developing contrasts like the one with which we began this section, between the billiard ball and the person who moves it, and claiming that there is no way of understanding these contrasts except in terms of this theory: billiard balls never directly cause anything to happen. A second main argument appeals to each agent's experience in acting. When I move my arm, I am aware before moving it that whether or not it moves is entirely up to me. In moving it, I am aware that it is moving because of me; somehow "I" am the explanation of its motion. Again, the theory is held to be the only plausible way of interpreting this awareness. Alternative theories seem to bypass the agents themselves, going directly from such things as desires or stimuli to the doing-related events that they cause.

On this theory it appears that my awareness of moving my arm is really awareness that I am directly causing some event which in turn causes the arm's motion. The directly caused event, then, or my directly causing it, is the source of the special awareness that I as an agent have of my action—the feature X we spoke of in the preceding section. And as anticipated, it appears both necessary and sufficient for action, at least on the supposition that it causes motion of my arm.

Theories like Taylor's are perennially attractive, but it should be understood that accepting such a theory involves paying a heavy price. Causation is a much-studied topic in metaphysics and the philosophy of science, and although many problems remain, some understanding has been achieved on the assumption that causation—the "cement of the universe," as one book refers to it—is a relation between events.[10] By contrast, direct causation of events by agents remains a mysterious, even *essentially* mysterious, phenomenon. How, for example, do we know that billiard balls do not directly cause anything to happen? Is it because we never see one move spontaneously? But perhaps when a cue stick hits, what happens is that impact of the cue stick causes the billiard ball to directly cause itself to move! And if we did see a billiard ball move spontaneously, how could we decide whether its motion was wholly un-

[10] Actually, philosophers disagree as to whether causes and effects are best thought of as events, states of affairs, conditions, or something else. John L. Mackie, *The Cement of the Universe* (Oxford: The Clarendon Press, 1974), seems to favor conditions. Donald Davidson is perhaps the leading exponent of causation as a relation strictly between events. See, for example, his "Causal Relations," *Journal of Philosophy* LXIV (1967), 691–703, reprinted in Ernest Sosa, ed., *Causation and Conditionals* (Oxford: Oxford University Press, 1975), pp. 82–94. Sosa's anthology also contains an article by Mackie, and a good collection of other views. In this book, I try to follow Davidson's approach.

caused, or directly caused by the billiard ball itself? Advocates of theories of agency have never provided good answers to these and similar questions. If the arguments can be resisted, then, we ought not to complicate our metaphysical picture of the universe and what transpires in it by admitting direct causation of events by agents.

And the arguments can be resisted, easily. There are many differences between persons and billiard balls that we can understand; we do not need to explain them in terms of one we do not understand. As for an agent's special awareness of acting, it is just that: awareness of acting. To claim that it is really awareness of directly causing some event is to assume what was to be argued. Yes, when I move my arm, I am aware that it is moving "because of me." But perhaps what this means is that its motion is caused by an event of a certain kind. We have been given no reason for rejecting the possibility that causation by an agent is compatible with and even explicable in terms of causation by events—contrary to the first passage quoted from Taylor.[11]

THE CONTEXTUAL THEORY   Inadequacy of the theories considered so far has led some to think it altogether wrongheaded to seek the nature of action in any kind of causation of doing-related events, especially causation by something "inner" This feeling is buttressed by the reflection that often enough, spectators can tell correctly whether what they observe is a case of action or "merely" the motion of a part of the body, despite their lack of access to anything "inside" the agent. Perhaps we would do better to attend to features available to spectators as well as agents—features which make up the context in which action takes place. Perhaps even the agent relies unconsciously on them, so that they, rather than anything internal, are the "features X," the source of the agent's special awareness.

Recall one of our earlier examples:

(b) Sue stepped on the brake when a child suddenly darted out in the path of the car.

Here the action is quite clearly embedded in a larger context of goal-directed and rule-governed activity. The agent is driving a car, an activity generally aimed at reaching some definite destination, and subject to a huge structure of formal and informal rules of the road. Understanding

[11] Roderick M. Chisholm, "Freedom and Action," in Keith Lehrer, ed., *Freedom and Determinism* (New York: Random House, Inc., 1966), pp. 28–44 (partly reprinted in Brand, *NHA*, pp. 283–92), defends a theory like Taylor's as implied by our belief that we are morally responsible for many of the things we do. But we will discuss responsibility in Chapter 6, and never come across a reason for introducing this theory. Recently Chisholm seems to have modified his position. See footnotes 21 and 22, below.

this, we can understand the motion of her foot against the pedal as fitting into a familiar pattern. The agent herself, having learned how to drive a car, is also sensitive to these features of her situation in the same way. On the one hand, she has been trained to react to children in situations like these with motion of her foot against the pedal. And on the other hand, she has in the same learning process been trained to see herself in such situations as stopping the car, and not simply as experiencing motion of her foot against the pedal. So oriented has the learning process made her to the most significant features of her activity and its context that she may even be unaware of which foot has moved against the pedal.

On this approach, the precise cues, external or internal, which lead the agent to awareness of acting are unimportant. Sue is aware that she is stopping the car and that the car is not merely stopping. If she is aware of her foot's motion, she believes she is moving it and that it is not "merely" moving. Perception of the child and the car's deceleration, sensory feedback from her foot and muscles, and her background knowledge of what driving a car is all about and what were the details of this trip in particular—all these factors and others may play some role in explaining her awareness. But what matters is the fact that what is happening does fit in with the larger pattern of a rational and trained agent driving a car in these circumstances. This is a pattern and a "fit" which others may be aware of as well as Sue, even if not in exactly the same ways, and it is what leads them also to the belief that the car is slowing down and that her foot moved as it did *because of her.*

The *contextual theory*, then, asserts that this pattern and fit, the features X of our previous discussions, are what makes it true that these events are occurring "because of her."[12] More officially:

(4) An agent has done an A, and his doing so was an action, just in case an E_A occurred in a context such that it fits into some intelligible (e.g., goal-oriented or rule-governed) pattern of activity in which the agent is engaged.

The "patterns of activity" into which events must "fit" are not all so definitely associated with goals and rules as is driving a car, as will be shown by an attempt to apply (4) to our other examples of action. But proponents of (4) claim that if an event's context really allows no way of viewing it as embedded in an intelligible pattern of activity, then it should *not* be regarded as occurring "because of the agent." If Sam's arm moves in his sleep, or even while he is awake but in a movie theater

12 Contextual theorists include A. I. Melden, *Free Action* (New York: Humanities Press, Inc., 1961); R. S. Peters, *The Concept of Motivation* (London: Routledge and Kegan Paul, 1958); and Joseph Margolis, *Knowledge and Existence* (New York: Oxford University Press, 1973), pp. 146–79. Gerald E. Zuriff, "Where Is the Agent in Behavior?" *Behaviorism* 3 (1975), 1–21, develops a theory of this kind, bringing insights and concepts of behaviorist psychology to bear.

wholly absorbed with the movie, we should not say "Sam has moved his arm." Or if we do say this, we should at least insist that it is a "mere" doing, not an action. One reason for this is that actions are things we can evaluate as well done, praiseworthy, foolish, and so on; but if the context supplies no relevant goal or rule, there is no standard by which to evaluate.

The theory may be incorrigibly vague at points, and there is an air of circularity about the formulation presented here: can we identify "patterns of activity in which the agent is engaged" without already knowing what the theory is supposed to tell us? But proponents could reply that the theory reflects accurately the concept of action that is embedded in our language and thought, a concept which *is* vague and incapable of being fully explained without circularity to someone not an agent, not already immersed in patterns of activity and awareness of that activity.

A more telling objection is that (4) would classify as cases of action some which should not be so classified. Suppose, for example, that Sue's foot moved against the pedal because of some sort of muscular spasm rather than because of the normal mechanism—but happened to do so at *exactly the same moment* as it would have if the normal mechanism had been operative. The event fits as well or as badly as before into the pattern of Sue's activity, judging by contextual features. So according to (4) she stopped the car, and there is no important difference between this case and the normal case. This seems patently false.[13]

It will be objected that she *did* stop the car, though not in the normal way. Still, it seems wrong to evaluate this alleged doing—certainly it would be wrong to credit *her* (or her driving skill) for it. And with additional stretches of our imagination, the example can be made more difficult for proponents of (4). The motion of her foot may have resulted from a tap on her knee administered surreptitiously by another passenger in the car. Or the passenger may have pressed a button to electrically jolt her muscles in just the right way; if the resulting motion is the result of anyone's doing at all, it is this passenger's, not Sue's. Perhaps the passenger's activity changes the context in a way of which an improved version of (4) would take note. Let us imagine then that Sue's muscles simply happened to contract, with nothing at all causing them to contract. (Nerve impulses which *would* have caused them to contract we may imagine short-circuited by some rare and temporary malfunction.) Now to all appearances, including Sue's own awareness, the context is normal. But though no one may realize it, Sue has *not* moved her foot and is *not* stopping the car. Contrary to the contextual theory, what happens inside the agent does matter.

---

[13] Davidson, "Actions, Reasons, and Causes," and Shaffer, *Philosophy of Mind*, p. 96, offer similar arguments.

THE VOLITIONAL Versions of the contextual theory appeal to phi-
THEORY losophers and psychologists suspicious of alleged
references to "inner" phenomena in the things we
say and believe about ourselves and others. Our beliefs are expressible in
language, and language is learned and taught publicly; how could such
references have crept in, or be important even if they are present? Elabo-
ration of this question and possible responses to it would entail a thorough survey of recent philosophy of language and philosophy of mind.
But it is now widely accepted that despite our ignorance of physiology,
and despite one person's lack of direct access to the contents of another's
mind, the things we say and believe may explicitly or implicitly commit
us to *postulating* certain kinds of phenomena which would explain things
closer to public observability. Perhaps I cannot feel or otherwise directly
perceive another's physical pain. But seeing him fall, watching him limp,
and hearing him complain, I readily accept the hypothesis that he is
complaining because he is indeed in a state of the kind called "pain." I
accept further that physiological mechanisms connecting leg to mind are
playing some sort of role, though I have no further knowledge of these
mechanisms or how they play their role. Likewise, if I believe another
has acted because I see his limb move, I am accepting a hypothesis about
something "inner"—an event, however, not a state—and an unknown
mechanism linking it to the limb's motion. This event shall be called a
volition. In the case of Sue just described, a volition may have occurred,
but the mechanism malfunctioned, and her leg's motion was independent of it. For this reason it is not true that she moved her leg.

The volitional theory, then, postulates "volitions," and asserts:

(5) An agent has done an A, and his doing an A is an action, just in case an E_A
occurred as the result of a volition of the agent's.

What kind of events volitions are may be understood by considering how
they explain what they are postulated to explain. These include at least
the connections between doing-related events and the antecedents of
action, and the special awareness agents have of their actions.

Sometimes an action is preceded by and occurs because of a desire.
Sometimes actions come from a sense of duty, perception of a situation
calling for action of a certain sort, strong emotion, or just sudden impulse. Now it is not enough for action that an antecedent of one of these
or similar kinds leads to an event of a doing-related type; it must do so in
the right way. What (5) implies is that the right way is *via* a volition.
Sometimes an action is preceded by nothing of the kinds mentioned, but
occurs simply from force of habit, or perhaps spontaneously, with no
antecedent of any kind. In such cases also there is a difference between

an action and mere occurrence of a doing-related event. According to (5), we have an action in these cases only if it is a volition which occurs "from force of habit" or "spontaneously," having a doing-related event as a result.

As for agents' awareness, it is explained by postulating volitions, since they are the features X of previous discussion. Consider a kind of experiment described by William James. "Close the patient's eyes, hold his anaesthetic arm still, and tell him to raise his hand to his head; and when he opens his eyes he will be astonished to find that the movement has not taken place."[14] Here the agent thought he had complied with the request. Why? The most natural explanation is that he had all the "awareness" he ever has when performing actions of this kind, except for whatever his eyes and the arm itself normally contribute. In other words, feature X was present and caused him to believe he was moving his arm as requested. Normally, when feature X causes such a belief, the agent *is* moving his arm, the awareness is genuine. Here, however, the arm did not move; it was held still. It is most plausible to suppose that the arm *would* have moved had it not been held still, and the cause of its motion would have been the very same thing which caused the agent's (mistaken) belief: feature X, what we are now calling a volition. A volition, then, is an event which is normally a cause of the agent's belief that he is acting in a certain way, *and* which normally causes such doing-related events as make it true that he *is* acting in that way.

**VOLITIONS,
ATTEMPTS,
AND MENTAL EVENTS**   Upon learning that the arm had not moved, the agent might say that he had *tried* to move it as requested, and that what he thought was awareness of actually moving it was merely awareness of this attempt. This leads to the suggestion that volitions are attempts.

Some object that attempts are not involved in every case of action as the volitional theory requires of volitions. People do not ordinarily "try" to move their arms, for example. To say so would imply that they used extra effort, or were uncertain whether they would succeed, or both of these.

Now the word "try" does often connote effort or doubt as to success or both; but this just shows we tend to reserve the *word* for cases of effort or doubt. The *phenomenon* of trying might still be present even where there is neither extra effort nor doubt. It even seems necessary to assume this; otherwise, how could we say in retrospect, when the arm fails to

14 William James, *The Principles of Psychology* (New York: Dover Publications, Inc., 1950), II, 105. See Bibliography for other literature on the volitional theory.

move, that the agent "tried but failed"? Finally, it has been pointed out that however strange it may be to say that agents normally "try" to move their arms and the like, it is stranger still to deny that they try, where the action is intentional. "I intentionally moved my arm, though in no way did I try to move it" seems to defy coherent interpretation.

Volitions are attempts, then, or a subclass of attempts; and in postulating them explicitly, the volitional theory is not really introducing anything new. Still, it will be useful on occasion to have a special verb in place of "trying," as we have "volition" in place of "attempt." We shall use "willing," a verb which, like "trying," has senses and connotations we will want to avoid, but which has a distinguished history of use in approximately the sense we want.

Volitions are attempts, and attempts—tryings—are *doings*. This contrasts with desires, which are *states:* we cannot use continuous tenses and say, for example, that Sam "was wanting" something. The point is worth noting, since some writers have considered accounts of the nature of action in terms of desires (and other mental states) as versions of the volitional theory. Objections we raised to those accounts earlier in this chapter are inadequate as objections to the volitional theory in the face of the reasons given why we *should* postulate volitions, and the evidence just presented that we *do* postulate them, in the guise of attempts.

Volitions do share an important feature with desires: they have *objects*. A volition (attempt) is a volition (attempt) *to do an A* for some act-type A, just as a desire is a desire to do something or to have something happen. All (or nearly all) mental phenomena have objects, in this sense of something they are directed toward or are somehow "about." My fear is aimed at the bear behind me, or the low grade I suspect I may get on a test; my thoughts are about my vacation plans; my perceptual experiences, for that matter, are about the things I perceive. A widespread view is that *only* mental phenomena have objects, and so volitions would also qualify as mental events.

It has in fact been suggested that volitions are *thoughts:* to will to move one's arm is to think of moving it (or to think of it moving) "in the executive mode." But this provides uncertain illumination, so long as we do not know what thoughts are, or understand what is meant by the executive mode, which distinguishes the special *kind* of thoughts that volitions are supposed to be.

A second hallmark of mental phenomena besides their having objects is their accessibility to consciousness, to the person's direct awareness. And it has been claimed that volitions are mental in this sense. On this view, we are aware or potentially aware of all our volitions, but they are *sui generis:* we cannot describe them or explain their nature in words.

But many objectors have asserted they are not aware of volitions in their own experience of acting; and the truth seems to be with them.[15] Volitions lead to awareness of the action one is performing, and awareness of the type of action one is willing (trying) to perform. The agent is not generally aware of the willing, the volition, in itself. Finally, even if an agent can focus his attention on his volition rather than on what he is succeeding in getting done, it does not seem that there are any *intrinsic features* of the volition of which he can become aware—features by which he might distinguish, for example, between a volition to move his arm and a volition to move his leg.[16]

VOLITIONS AS FUNCTIONALLY CHARACTERIZED

Perhaps comparing them to other mental phenomena or searching for their intrinsic features is not the way to understand better what volitions are. Rather we should develop further the remark on page 16: "A volition is an event which is normally a cause of the agent's belief that he is acting in a certain way, and which normally causes such doing-related events as make it true that he is acting in that way." This is the germ of a *functional characterization* of volitions, a description of the ways in which they are related to other events and states of the agent, mental and nonmental. For that matter, many philosophers believe that functional characterizations are what is needed to best understand mental phenomena of *all* kinds.[17]

One dimension omitted in the quoted remark was also touched upon earlier: the fact that volitions mediate between doing-related events and such antecedents of action as Sam's desire to move his arm, Sue's perception of the child in front of the car, and so on. An attempt to list all of these, and spell out in detail all the relations characteristic of volitions, would probably fail or be too complex to be intelligible. But a fairly precise formulation of the three dimensions we have, followed by some comments, may help round out such insight as we have attained into the nature of action.

Our formulation (5) of the volitional theory provides that an agent has done an A if an E_A occurs as the result of a volition; but this need not be a volition *to do an A*. The E_A may have been an accidental conse-

---

[15] The "classical" source for this and other objections to the volitional theory is Gilbert Ryle, *The Concept of Mind* (New York: Barnes & Noble, Inc., 1949; London: Hutchinson & Company, Ltd., 1949), pp. 62–69, reprinted in Brand, *NHA*, pp. 61–66. Another of Ryle's objections is discussed later in this chapter, and a third in the next chapter.

[16] This point has been developed as an objection to the volitional theory by Melden, *Free Action*, chap. 5.

[17] See Bibliography for more on this view.

quence. If a volition mediated between Sam's desire to move his arm and motion of the arm, then Sam has moved his arm, and his doing so was an action. Perhaps the volition had "moving one's arm" as its object. But suppose the arm hit a vase, causing it to fall and break. *Sam* broke the vase and his doing so was an action (presumably unintentional, but this is irrelevant now), since its breaking was caused by Sam's volition (via causing the arm's motion). But it would be odd to suppose that the volition had "breaking the vase" as its object.

In the next chapter we will consider the puzzling relation holding among doings like Sam's volition, his moving his arm, and his breaking the vase. Our immediate concern is to provide a functional characterization of a volition which does have the act-type A as its object. How shall we decide which act-types are the objects of volitions?

Consider how an agent goes about doing an A when he has been requested to do so, or has realized that he has some other reason for doing so. Often he will need to decide upon means. Had Sam been asked to break the vase, he might have thought: "I can break it by moving my arm against it, forcefully." This thought expresses a belief he had about how to perform an action of the type in question. Without this belief or another about some other way to break the vase (e.g., by kicking it), Sam would have had no idea what to do. Whatever he ended up doing might or might not have chanced to lead to the vase's breaking.

Now suppose Sam is asked simply to move his arm. He does not need to decide upon means. He may or may not have a belief about how he moves his arm, or can move it. He may believe he moves his arm by contracting certain muscles in his shoulder, or he may not even know that he *has* muscles. Either way, it is likely that the right muscles will contract so that his arm moves.

This contrast leads us to say that "moving one's arm" can be the object of a volition in Sam, while "breaking a vase" cannot. Suppose that in either of the cases described a volition actually occurred which caused Sam's arm to move against the vase, with the further result that the vase fell and broke. This volition was directed at getting the arm to move; Sam tried (successfully) to move his arm. In the second case, that is the whole story. In the first case, where Sam was asked to break the vase, we may say he *tried* to break it. (Again, the attempt was successful.) But this is so only because of the role played by Sam's belief about how to break the vase. In itself, the volition was directed simply at getting the arm to move. The volition's object was the act-type "moving one's arm," and this is shown by the irrelevance to its occurrence of any belief Sam may have had about how to perform an action of this type. (In a more detailed and rigorous version of the volitional theory, we might find reason to specify the volition's object as something like "moving one's right arm so it pushes against the object at such-and-such position in one's visual field." But we shall not go so far in this book.)

A volition to do an A, then, is an event which:

(a) is likely to occur when and only when the agent wants or has other reason (see below) to do an A; and if the agent has any beliefs about how he does or can do an A, it would be as likely to occur even if he lacked them;
(b) normally directly causes (or directly contributes to causing) the agent to believe that he is doing an A (or, in cases where the agent has reason for uncertainty, that he is *trying* to do an A); and
(c) normally causes an E_A.

If a volition to do an A occurs in an agent, then the agent has *willed to do an A*.

The reference to "other reason" in (a) is necessary since we recognize that actions may have antecedents other than desires. There might be an agent in whom a volition to do an A would not be likely to occur however much he wanted to do an A, but would be likely to occur if, for example, he thought he was obligated to do an A. The phrase "other reason" should be understood as broadly as possible. Even so, we also recognize the possibility of actions occurring with *no* preceding desire or other reason; hence the word "likely."

The "normally" in (b) and (c) similarly allows for abnormal cases where an agent wills to do an A but fails, since no E_A occurs as a result and the agent is even unaware of having made the attempt, since the volition failed to cause belief that he was doing an A (or even trying). The word is misleading, however, since it suggests that a volition to do an A causes the indicated belief and event *most of the time*. Perhaps the agent hardly ever wills to do an A, and each time he does, something goes wrong to block the belief or the event or both! We could not say in his case that the volition to do an A is an event which normally causes the belief and the event.

Less misleading would be "would cause in normal circumstances"; it would then be necessary to explain what circumstances are "normal" so far as (b) and (c) are concerned. A case in which the agent does an A from habit and at the time is wholly engrossed in something else might be abnormal in that his volition produces no belief that he is doing an A. (Or is there belief, but just no awareness in the sense of conscious thought?) An event of type E_A would fail to occur if at the time the agent was physiologically unable to do an A, or if the setting was one in which an event of type E_A was physically impossible. But these notions themselves need to be clarified and probably do not cover all that is needed to eliminate the vagueness of (c). We shall not try to improve matters.[18]

[18] But see Chapter 3, below, and Goldman, *THA*, pp. 64–66.

The word "directly" in (b) is meant to rule out causation of the belief via causation of an event of type E_A. A volition in Sam might cause his arm to move; he might see and feel it moving and infer that he is moving it. If perception and inference are causal processes, this is a way in which the volition *indirectly* causes the belief. But the whole point of the case described by James is that an agent may come to believe he is moving his arm even if he does *not* see or feel it moving. The volition causes the belief directly. (It may be noted that without this requirement in (b), (b) would be true of the muscle contractions which cause Sam's arm to move when he moves it; and (a) and (c) as they stand seem also to be true of these contractions. But we would not want to conclude that these muscle contractions constitute Sam's volition to move his arm.)

Enough has now been said about the nature of volitions to enable consideration of an important objection to (5). According to (5), if an event occurs as the result of an agent's volition, then the agent has performed some action. (We assume the event is of a type corresponding to some act-type, an E_A for some A.) No constraints are placed on *how* the volition causes the event. Now, we objected on precisely this ground to (2), the view that for action it is sufficient that a doing-related event occur because of a desire. Desire and event must be connected in what Goldman called a "certain characteristic way," and which we understood as via feature X. Feature X has now turned out to be a volition, an event of which (a), (b), and (c) are true. But perhaps this is still not enough. Perhaps the volition also must be connected to the event in the right way.

This objection is unfounded. Desires and volitions differ in a crucial respect: the latter, but not the former, are *doings*. So long as a volition occurs, the agent has already "done" something. If an E_A occurs as a result, it occurs as the result of something the agent has done, and this allows us to say he has "done an A." Since what led to the E_A was not just any doing but a volition, an event of the kind crucial to understanding action, we can say the agent's doing an A was itself an action. The agent's doing an A may have been entirely unintentional; the agent may even have had no idea that he was doing an A. But this is irrelevant. Unintentional and unwitting actions are still actions.

Notice it does not matter what the object of the volition is. Suppose Sam wills to move his arm—that is, a volition occurs whose object is "moving one's arm." Unknown to Sam, however, some diabolical neurophysiologist has during Sam's surgery the previous day "rewired" Sam's nerves, so that as a result of the volition, his *leg* moves. Sam has moved his leg, and his doing so was an action—unintentional to be sure! Or suppose the volition does lead to motion of the arm, but not in a "normal" way. At an extreme, we can suppose the nerves to the muscles severed, and reintroduce the mind reader of our discussion of (2). Noticing occurrence of the volition, the mind reader obligingly moves Sam's arm for him. Had Sam not willed to move his arm, the mind reader would not have done anything, so the mind reader's action, hence the motion of Sam's arm, occurred as a result of Sam's volition. It follows in accordance with (5) that Sam has moved his arm, and that his doing so was an action. (Perhaps we should not say he "moved his arm," but only that he "got it to move." Still, his getting his arm to move was an action.) Here it is harder to decide what, if anything, Sam has done "intentionally"; but again, this is a separate question. The objection to (5) is unsuccessful.

EVENT OR PROCESS? The impression given so far is no doubt that volitions are brief events which entirely precede the awareness and doing-related events which they cause. Sam wills to raise his arm, *and then* the arm goes up, and (simultaneously) he comes to believe that he is raising his arm. Between volition and arm-motion various neural and muscular events intervene, but these also apparently occur after the volition, which is over and done with once Sam has initiated his action. But this picture of volitions may be seriously misleading.

Volitions have objects which are act-types like "raising one's arm." To succeed in performing an action of this type and most others, a certain *end-state* must be reached—e.g., a state in which the arm is up. The bodily changes which a volition "normally" causes can be expected "normally" to bring about this end-state; a volition to raise one's arm does not normally cause muscles of the leg to contract! But more happens than simple triggering of the normally appropriate muscular events. Processes are initiated which may be said to "monitor" the progress of the arm's motion. If unexpected resistance is encountered, greater effort will be exerted. When the arm reaches the "up" state, further contraction of the muscles will be arrested (and other muscles may be brought into play) to bring the arm's motion to a smooth halt. The degree to which these adjustments are conscious is a complicated question; but our concern now is whether some or all of the monitoring processes should be regarded as part of the volition. If they are so regarded, then a volition to raise one's arm is not a brief event preceding the arm's motion, but a continuing process which may last as long as that motion, and in some sense controls it. Volitions having other act-types as their objects would presumably also include monitoring processes and would last until the relevant end-state is achieved or the attempt to bring it about is given up.

Other types of action reveal even greater complexity. Consider casual conversation between two friends. Is each remark made by each participant a separate action? What if a remark consists of several sentences or several paragraphs? Shall we hypothesize a separate volition for each sentence, or just one volition whose object is "to remark that . . ."? What if one speaker interrupts the other in mid-sentence and then the first speaker resumes? Has a brand-new volition occurred?

Gilbert Ryle thought the perplexity of questions like these constituted an argument against the very hypothesis that there *are* volitions. (He asked how many "acts of will" a person "executes in, say, reciting 'Little Miss Muffet' backwards.")[19] But suppose we think of volitions as ongoing processes. When a person begins conversing with another, a volitional process is initiated. Perhaps we can even say of it that its object is "conversing." It is a kind of process which is "likely to occur if the agent wants to converse; causes the agent to believe that he is conversing; and causes doing-related events such that he is in fact conversing." As for the particular remarks that are made and thoughts that are expressed, these are "controlled" by this volitional process as it "monitors" the course of the conversation. The manner of expression would also be controlled: choice of words and sentence structure, temporary halts and resumptions after being interrupted, and so on. Exactly how the volitional process controls the agent's conversational output—how it is determined just what is to be said—will depend on the agent's beliefs and attitudes as well as the physical circumstances of the conversation, making this example more complicated than that of raising one's arm. It will be possible and tempting to treat portions of the volitional process as volitions in their own right, having more specific objects than "conversing." But there may be no single, best way of dividing up the process into such "subvolitions," and so no definite answers to the questions of the preceding paragraph. This is no more an argument against the existence of volitions than is a similar difficulty in dividing a range into discrete mountains an argument against the existence of mountains.

THE LOCATION OF VOLITIONS Volitions are mental events, so they occur "in the mind." But where is this? According to the *dualist* theory of René Descartes and most of its modern versions, the mind is a nonmaterial substance associated with the body (especially the brain) of the person whose mind it is, but not really located anywhere in that body or anywhere at all. Nonmaterial things are nonspatial.

According to *materialist* theories, there are no nonmaterial things of this kind. There are three main possibilities: (1) the mind is in fact the

[19] Ryle, *The Concept of Mind*, p. 65. Copyright 1949 by Gilbert Ryle. Courtesy of Barnes and Noble Books (Div. of Harper and Row Publishers, Inc.) and the Hutchinson Publishing Group, Ltd.

brain (or some other portion of the body); (2) the mind is just the whole person viewed in a certain way; or (3) the mind is something which if we spoke most accurately, we would not speak of at all (just as we might not speak of the sun "rising" and "setting," to avoid suggesting that *it* moves rather than the earth). If (1) is correct, then volitions are actually bodily events—perhaps brain processes of various complicated sorts—and are located in the relevant parts of the body. (They would probably not all be brain processes of the same sort, since people differ in the ways the neurons in their brains are interconnected, and even in the same person the pattern changes as the person develops.) If (2) or (3) is correct, the best answer we can give to the question of where volitions occur is "wherever the person is"; and this may be where the *whole* body is, not any smaller region.[20]

Our account of volitions is compatible with dualism and with each of these three possibilities. Nothing in (a), (b), or (c) entails that volitions are either material or nonmaterial phenomena. They are capable of causing beliefs and doing-related events, and the latter include some material phenomena (e.g., the motion of an arm). But most philosophers today agree that even if mental events are nonmaterial, they can have material effects. A materialist who thinks (1) is correct might even use our characterization to support his view: he might gather evidence that (a), (b), and (c) were true of certain events in the brain and then claim that these events were volitions. But our characterization is admittedly incomplete; perhaps to really be a volition, an event would have to have some fourth thing true of it which is true of no event in the brain or other portion of the body. We will briefly mention one suggestion along these lines, which, if correct, points in the direction of (2) or (3).

Volitions have objects, something they are "about" or "for." A volition to move one's arm has as its object the act-type "moving one's arm"; a volition to stop the car (if there are any) has as its object "stopping the car"; and so on. Do (a), (b), and (c) capture this feature of volitions?

The act-type A enters our characterization through the relation between it and the event-type E_A, as part of the object (or "content") of the agent's belief, and as the object of the desire which according to (a) may be present. If this is enough to show that the volition to do an A itself has A for its object, then we have explained what it is for an event of one kind—a volition—to have a certain object in terms of its relations with events (actually, states—but we could reformulate in terms of the agent's *coming* to believe, desire, and so on) of other kinds. The possibility of doing this has been explicitly denied by Roderick Chisholm in

---

[20] For an elementary survey of dualist and materialist theories, see Shaffer, *Philosophy of Mind,* or Keith Campbell, *Body and Mind* (Garden City, N.Y.: Anchor Books, 1970).

the course of developing an account of action in terms of "undertakings" otherwise comparable to our account in terms of "volitions."[21] If he is right, then (a), (b), and (c) are seriously inadequate as a characterization of volitions.

We cannot explore the pros and cons of Chisholm's position, which is one side of an ongoing controversy in recent philosophy. If he is right, the simplest way to repair our characterization would be to add "(d) has A as its object"—something to which we are committed anyway—to (a), (b), and (c).

One element of his position, however, seems to be that the properties of events and states with *objects* cannot be fully explained or understood without mentioning the persons or other beings which are their *subjects* —the ones who do the wanting, trying, believing, and so on.[22] And this may imply that no event which has an object can be identified with an event located "merely" in the brain or other portion of the whole person. That is, the thrust of Chisholm's position as it bears on the location of volitions is toward (2) or (3) rather than (1), and toward the view that volitions are located "wherever the person is." Chisholm, in fact, suggests that our "undertakings," as he calls them, could be events in the brain "only if we ourselves are identical with our brain or with some proper part of our brain."[23]

CONCLUSION   The question of this chapter was how can we distinguish actions from other doings. The answer at which we have arrived is given by (5), the volitional theory: a doing of type A is an action if and only if the event of the corresponding type E_A occurs as the result of a volition. (This presupposes that the type A does have a corresponding type E_A, but in this chapter we are not considering any exceptions to this.) Hiccupping, bleeding, and other doings we men-

---

[21] Roderick M. Chisholm, "The Agent as Cause," in Myles Brand and Douglas Walton, eds., *Action Theory* (Dordrecht: D. Reidel Publishing Company, 1976), pp. 199–211. One difference between Chisholm's theory and the one developed here is that according to Chisholm, the agent causes his undertakings. We have not claimed that the agent causes his volitions, and it seems that normally he does not, at least not intentionally. One interesting class of exceptions includes cases of self-control. In these, the agent deliberately gets himself to do something—for example, by committing himself to do it, by resisting an impulse to do something else, perhaps even by *willing* to get himself to do it. See footnote 18 in Chapter 4 and also pp. 82 and 127.

[22] If this is indeed Chisholm's view, it is closely related to Richard Taylor's view of events "directly caused" by agents. But Taylor does not say that directly caused events have objects. It is not clear whether Taylor believes there are events which are the *direct causings*, by the agent, of directly caused events. If he does, his position may be indistinguishable from Chisholm's.

[23] Chisholm, "The Agent as Cause," p. 211; see footnote 14 there.

tioned at the outset may safely be supposed not to occur as the result of any volitions, so they are not actions—although if we came across a person who tended to hiccup when and only when he had reason to and who seemed to have awareness of his hiccupping not entirely due to feedback from his respiratory system, we would have reason to think that *his* hiccupping, or many instances of it, were actions.

There is a subtlety here. Imagine Sam is running down the field; he stumbles. If he had not been running, he would not have stumbled. This may allow us to say his running caused his stumbling. But the motions of his legs in running were caused by volitions, so these volitions caused his stumbling. Must we say that his stumbling was an action? No. We must bear in mind the distinction between an act-type A and the corresponding event-type E_A. Sam's stumbling would be an action if we could isolate an event-type which would correspond to "stumbling" as, say, "motion of one's arm" corresponds to "moving one's arm." It does not seem we can do this. Rather, what we can say is that "stumbling" itself is an event-type corresponding in this way to "getting oneself to stumble." We *can* say that Sam did something of this latter type, and there is no reason to deny that it was an action. By running, Sam did get himself to stumble—unintentionally of course, but unintentional actions are still actions.

Parallel to this distinction between "stumbling" and "getting oneself to stumble," we should distinguish between "hiccupping" and "getting oneself to hiccup." The agent we described whose hiccupping is often an action should be understood as *getting* himself to hiccup on these occasions. We need not *say* it this way, since the word "hiccupping" itself would naturally be understood in this context as "getting oneself to hiccup." Similarly, "Sam coughed" reports an event of a certain sort in Sam's respiratory tract, but in certain contexts—e.g., where the cough was deliberate—it might also carry the implication that the event in his respiratory tract was caused by a volition. In the latter case, Sam has performed an action, of the type "getting oneself to cough." If no volition was involved, Sam's coughing was a mere doing. The words "Sam coughed" might be used to cover either case.

CHAPTER TWO

Actions
and Events

TWO PROBLEMS   Sue tells Sam how she handled the traffic emergency; a volition then occurs in Sam, causing his vocal apparatus to produce a sound we represent as "vĕ rĕ gŏŏd." According to the volitional theory and what we surmise of the situation, Sam has said "Very good!" and his doing so was an action. But how are these three—the volition, the sound, and the action—related to one another? The first caused the second; did it also cause the third? Perhaps the action—"what Sam did"—*is* the sound he produced, the effect his volition had in the observable world. Alternatively, both the sound and the volition may be *parts* of the action; since volitions are mental events, on this conception actions bridge the gap between mental and physical. Finally, it may be that Sam's action is neither more nor less than his volition; human actions are to be understood as mental events, even though we often describe them in ways implying that they have certain physical effects.

Each of these positions on the parts, antecedents, and consequences of actions has its supporters. The arguments are bound up with arguments on a related problem, that of the *individuation* of actions. Our example illustrates this second problem if we reflect that by saying "Very good!" Sam praised Sue, and most likely made her happy with this praise. Is this one action he performed, two, or three? "Saying 'Very good!'" "praising Sue," and "making Sue happy" are three different *types* of action. Is this enough to warrant saying Sam performed three different actions, or shall we say Sam performed one action exemplifying all three types? Perhaps he performed two actions here, one which did and one which did not involve a change in Sue. Again, each answer has its supporters.

Resolution of these problems matters first of all to metaphysicians, who are concerned with the nature and place of events generally among the items making up the universe, and concerned with actions in particular as a specially interesting subclass of events. It matters also to others concerned with precision in thinking and talking about human behavior. Psychologists cannot claim both to deal with actions and to limit themselves to publicly observable phenomena, if the truth is that actions are wholly or partly mental. And discussions of the morality of abortion are not helped by persisting uncertainty as to whether a doctor's saving the mother by killing the fetus is one action or two, each to be judged separately. Whether the uncertainty can be removed and the other questions answered in a fully satisfactory way is itself none too clear. In this chapter we shall survey the main lines of argument and adopt a tentative position.

IDENTITY We begin with the problem of individuation.

How can we decide whether or not Sam's praising Sue and his making her happy were one and the same action? Central to the argumentation is a principle about identity often called "Leibniz's Law," which we can formulate as:

x and *y* are *identical* if and only if every property of *x* is a property of *y*, and every property of *y* is a property of *x*.

This principle holds for every genuine property—including relational ones—and for everything we might substitute for *x* and *y*. Consider, for example, substituting "the father of Leif Ericson" for *x* and "Eric the Red" for *y*. The principle then implies that the father of Leif Ericson is identical with Eric the Red only if every property of the father of Leif Ericson is a property of Eric the Red, and vice versa. In this case, the condition is satisfied. The father of Leif Ericson had a son named Leif— and Eric the Red had a son named Leif. Eric the Red had red hair—and the father of Leif Ericson had red hair. And so on. The two phrases in fact refer to one and the same person, each reflecting a different way in which he was known. Similarly, anyone claiming that Sam's praising Sue and his making her happy were one and the same action would have to argue that the two phrases, "Sam's praising Sue" and "Sam's making her happy," refer in this context to one and the same action. They merely reflect two different ways of picking out this single action of Sam's: one in terms of the verbal content of the action, and the other in terms of the effect this same action had on Sue. On the other side, someone claiming that the two phrases in this example refer to two distinct actions would have to argue that there is at least one property of the action referred to by the one phrase which is not a property of the action referred to by the other phrase.

SEVEN ARGUMENTS   One genuine difference would be enough to show that Sam's praising Sue and his making her happy were distinct actions; but advocates of what we shall call the *prolific theory of individuation* have claimed to find at least seven kinds of difference in parallel examples.[1] Two can be illustrated here if we assume that Sam in fact had wanted to make Sue *unhappy* and was under the mistaken impression that praise always upset her:

(1) Sam's praising Sue was *intentional*, but his making her happy was not intentional.

(2) Sam's praising Sue is *explained* by his desire to make her unhappy and his belief that praising her would do this, but his making her happy is not explained by these.

Five more do not require such an assumption:

(3) Sam's praising Sue was in itself a *morally neutral* action, but his making her happy was in itself a morally good action (on the assumption that adding to another's happiness is always morally good in itself).

(4) Sam's praising Sue was *followed by* her becoming happy, but his making her happy was not followed by her becoming happy.

(5) Sam's praising Sue *caused* her to become happy, but his making her happy did not cause her to become happy.

(6) Sam's praising Sue was *done in English,* but his making her happy was not done in English.

---

[1] Several of these are discussed in Alvin I. Goldman, *A Theory of Human Action* (Englewood Cliffs, N.J.: Prentice-Hall, Inc., 1970; Princeton Paperback, 1976), pp. 1–10. (Hereafter referred to as *THA*.)

(7) Sam's praising Sue was *not done by* praising her, but his making her happy was done by praising her.

Each of these statements seems to be true. In support of (4), for example, note that we can say "Sam praised Sue and then she became happy," but "Sam made Sue happy and then she became happy" sounds wrong. And in each of the seven, the italicized word or phrase apparently indicates a property which Sam's praising Sue had but which his making her happy lacked. (In (2), (4), (5), and (7), the property is relational.) The nonidentity of the two seems amply established.

Sam's saying "Very good!" seems as different from his making Sue happy as does his praising her. But we cannot find all seven differences between his saying "Very good!" and his praising her. Both seem equally intentional and equally well explained by Sam's desire and belief. Both were morally neutral and "done in English." Both seem to have occurred during precisely the same interval of time, and it seems correct to say of each that it caused the change in Sue. But the seventh difference remains: Sam praised Sue by saying "Very good!" but he did not say "Very good!" by saying "Very good!" Assuming it is genuine, this one difference is again enough to show they are not one but two distinct actions.

THE PROLIFIC THEORY

How must we conceive of actions in order to understand Sam's saying "Very good!" and his praising Sue as being distinct? The only difference we found was in the property "done by saying 'Very good!'" In other properties they are alike: they had the same agent, Sam; they occurred simultaneously; they apparently had the same causes and the same effects; they involved the same parts of Sam's body.

Advocates of the prolific theory of individuation tend to an abstract conception of actions and events in general. The type of an action is regarded as a property of the agent; the action itself is the agent's exemplifying that property at the time. If the agent exemplifies two such properties at the same time, then there are two exemplifyings-by-him of properties, which is to say there are two distinct actions. A single action cannot then be of more than one type. There is a problem of how types are to be individuated. Is "praising Sue" the same type as "praising someone," or "praising a woman"?[2] We shall not try to solve this problem. But Sam's saying "Very good!" his praising Sue, and his making her happy are fairly clearly of three different types, and so according to the prolific theory they are three distinct actions.

[2] Goldman would say no, because "praising someone" is not synonymous with "praising Sue." See pp. 12–15 of *THA*.

GENERATION A pair of actions having the same agent and so on but differing in type are rather intimately related, even if we accept the view of the prolific theory that they are two distinct actions. Alvin Goldman has developed an account of this relation, which he calls *generation,* from the point of view of the prolific theory.[3] The relation is approximately that expressed by the word "by" in statement (7) and in:

(8) Sam praised Sue by saying "Very good!"

We say: Sam's praising Sue *generated* his making her happy, and his saying "Very good!" *generated* his praising her. The relation is transitive: if an agent did an A by doing a B and did a B by doing a C, then he did an A by doing a C. Here, Sam made Sue happy by saying "Very good!" and so we say that his saying "Very good!" generated his making her happy. The relation is also asymmetric and irreflexive: if an agent did an A by doing a B, he did *not* do a B by doing an A, nor did he do a B by doing a B. This is the point of statement (7) as an argument for the prolific theory. Sam did *not* praise Sue by making her happy, and neither did he say "Very good!" by praising her. His praising Sue was not generated by his making her happy, and did **not** generate his saying "Very good!"

Generation is easily confused with the means–end relation: notice that saying "Very good!" may well have been Sam's means to the end of praising Sue. But we can also suppose that he did not praise her *in order to* make her happy. It would then be misleading or just incorrect to say that praising Sue was his means to making her happy. Still, the former did generate the latter. Not every case of generation is a case of means and end. The two relations overlap, but are distinct.

Generation must also be distinguished carefully from the cause–effect relation. It is easy to make the mistake of thinking that Sam's praising Sue caused his making her happy; but this is a mistake. What Sam's praising Sue caused is the change in Sue, the event of her becoming happy. This event was not Sam's action at all.[4]

3 Goldman, *THA,* pp. 20–48. Goldman also calls the relation *level-generation,* because he employs diagrams representing actions standing in this relation as being at different levels. We can present only highlights of his discussion and shall deal only with the simplest, least problematic cases. For example, we shall not discuss the relation between Sam's making Sue happy and his pleasing Sue's mother, where he did *both* by saying "Very good!"

4 If it were, we should be able to say that Sam praised Sue and then made her happy, since we can say he praised her and then she became happy. Arthur C. Danto and Monroe C. Beardsley are among the philosophers who would disagree. See the former's *Analytical Philosophy of Action* (Cambridge: Cambridge University Press, 1973), p. 7, and the latter's "Actions and Events: The Problem of Individuation," *American Philosophical Quarterly,* 12 (1975), 263–76. Beardsley's article is a good survey of the whole issue, with many references to the literature.

What we can say in this example is that Sam's praising Sue *causally generated* his making her happy. An agent's doing a B causally generated his doing an A if the following two conditions are met:

1. the agent's doing a B caused an event of type E_A; and

2. the act-type A is "bringing about an event of type E_A."

Sam's praising Sue caused an event of the type "Sue's becoming happy," and the act-type "making Sue happy" just *is* "bringing about an event of the type 'Sue's becoming happy.'" (Condition 2 can be regarded as satisfied by all our examples.)

As a second example, consider the likely relation of Sam's dialing a California number to his making a phone ring in California. His doing the former caused the phone to ring, and so it causally generated his making the phone ring. But his dialing the California number did not cause his making the phone ring, nor did it causally generate the phone's ringing.

Not all generation is causal generation: the relation of Sam's saying "Very good!" to his praising Sue is a case in point. Praising Sue involved production of no event not involved in saying "Very good!" Rather what made it the case that Sam praised Sue are certain circumstances of his saying "Very good!" Among these are the conventions of the English language by which these words can indeed serve as an expression of praise, and the fact that Sam uttered them in an appropriate frame of mind (e.g., he was not speaking sarcastically).[5]

The occurrence of an event of a certain type as the effect of an action may also be viewed as a circumstance of the action, permitting a unified account of both causal and noncausal generation. If an agent's doing a B generated his doing an A, then it is true that he did an A because it is true that he did a B and that certain further circumstances obtained; but not vice versa. Sam's praising Sue generated his making her happy. What makes it true that he did the latter is that he did the former and his doing so was attended by the change in Sue as a result. But there were no further circumstances which, added to his making Sue happy, made it the case that he praised her. Similarly, Sam's saying "Very good!" plus the conventions of English and Sam's frame of mind made it the case that he praised her; but nothing *added* to his praising her made it the case that he said "Very good!"

As mentioned, this account of generation—the "by" relation of (7) and (8)—is from the point of view of the prolific theory. In the absence of any alternative account from a different point of view, this one strengthens (7) as an argument for that theory.

[5] The kind of *noncausal* generation exemplified here is only one of several distinguished and discussed by Goldman.

Many writers are unhappy with the prolific theory precisely because it proliferates the number of actions performed by an agent on a given occasion. Aside from the three actions we have been discussing, the theory is also committed to regarding each of the following as a distinct action performed by Sam: his uttering two English words, his saying something to Sue, his changing her mood, and so on, indefinitely. There is no clear limit to the number of distinct actions performed by Sam on this occasion according to this theory. Are these not too many to be believed?

An alternative theory enjoying considerable popularity in effect sees the distinction between causal and noncausal generation as crucial. Where according to the prolific theory, one action causally generates another, this *moderate theory* agrees that there are two actions. Sam's making Sue happy was *not* the same action as his praising her. But where the prolific theory implies that one action noncausally generates another, the moderate theory insists that there is only one action. Sam's praising Sue was the very same action as his saying "Very good!" Contrary to the position represented by the prolific theory, it is supposed to be possible for a single action to be of more than one type.[6]

There is a straightforward picture underlying the moderate theory, embodying a position on the other of the two problems with which this chapter began, that of the parts, antecedents, and consequences of actions. Recall statement (4) from our list of seven, which asserted in part that Sam's making Sue happy was not followed by her becoming happy. This was supported by the evident oddity of saying "Sam made Sue happy and then she became happy." But what does this oddity suggest? Think of events (including actions) as made up of smaller events, just as objects such as buildings are composed of smaller objects such as bricks which are their parts. A natural answer, then, is that her becoming happy—the change in Sue—was *part of Sam's action*. Similar reasoning shows it was not the only part: "Sam praised Sue and then made her happy" is misleading if the truth is that he made her happy *by* praising her, and this suggests that his praising her was also a part of his action of making her happy. That latter action consisted, then, in the smaller action of praising her together with an effect of that smaller action, and perhaps other events in between. The effect—the change in Sue—was

---

[6] For versions of this moderate theory, see Beardsley, "Actions and Events"; Lawrence H. Davis, "Individuation of Actions," *Journal of Philosophy*, LXVII (1970), 520–30; Judith J. Thomson, "The Time of a Killing," *Journal of Philosophy*, LXVIII (1971), 115–32, and *Acts and Other Events* (Ithaca and London: Cornell University Press, 1977); Hugh McCann, "Is Raising One's Arm a Basic Action?" *Journal of Philosophy*, LXIX (1972), 235–49; and Vivian Weil and Irving Thalberg, "The Elements of Basic Action," *Philosophia*, 4 (1974), 111–38. The last-mentioned article is the basis for chapter 5 of Irving Thalberg, *Perception, Emotion, and Action* (Oxford: Basil Blackwell, 1977).

merely a consequence of the smaller action, but literally a part of the larger.[7]

By contrast, there is no motivation for saying some event was part of Sam's praising Sue but not part of his saying "Very good!" or vice versa. It sounds odd to say "Sam said 'Very good!' and then there was the sound of his voice," so the moderate theory implies that the sound he produced is a part of his action of saying "Very good!" But it also sounds odd to say "Sam praised Sue and then there was the sound of his voice," suggesting that the sound was also part of his action of praising Sue. In fact every part of his praising Sue seems to have been part of his saying "Very good!" The further circumstances which made his saying "Very good!" a case of his praising Sue included the conventions of English and his frame of mind at the time; but these are not events that he brought about, so we have no reason to call them "parts" of his action. But then his praising Sue and his saying "Very good!" had all and only the same parts, implying that they are identical. A single one of the actions he performed on this occasion was of the type "saying 'Very good!'" and also of the type "praising someone."

Attractive as the underlying picture may be, proponents of this moderate theory must contend with the seven arguments we offered in behalf of the prolific theory. This is not as formidable a task as it may initially seem, however. Inspection reveals that the moderate theory can accept the arguments implicit in statements (4), (5), and probably (6), for they can only be applied where causal generation is involved, and in such cases the moderate theory agrees that the actions are not identical.

Of the remaining arguments, that suggested by (1) is widely agreed to be unsuccessful. The thrust of (1) is that Sam's making Sue happy and his praising her are not identical because they differ in respect of the property of "being intentional": Sam's praising Sue had this property, and his making her happy lacked it. But "being intentional" is not a genuine property, at least not without further specification. As we shall see, to say that an action is intentional is approximately to say something about how the action relates to certain of the agent's beliefs about the action and its circumstances. We have not fully specified the property until we indicate the content of the relevant beliefs, until we say just how the agent thought of the action. To say "Sam intentionally praised Sue" is, roughly, to say "Sam praised Sue and thought of this action as of the type 'praising Sue.'" To say "Sam intentionally made Sue happy" is, roughly, to say "Sam made Sue happy and thought of this action as of the type 'making Sue happy.'" But now we see that we cannot conclude

---

[7] According to the prolific theory, actions and events do not seem to have parts in this literal sense. Cf. Goldman, *THA*, p. 29.

from (1) that Sam's praising Sue is not identical with his making her happy. For the more fully specified property of Sam's action of praising Sue is "thought of by Sam as of the type 'praising Sue.'" And without additional argument, we have no reason for saying that Sam's action of making Sue happy lacked this very same property! Sam made Sue happy, a dissenter might claim, and he thought of this action simply as of the type "praising Sue."

The arguments implicit in (2), (3), and (7) can be countered in similar fashion. An explanation of an event is always an explanation of an event of a certain type. What (2) really means, then, is that Sam's desire and belief suffice to explain why an action of his occurred which was of the type "praising Sue," but do not suffice to explain why an action of his occurred which was of the type "making her happy." We cannot infer that there was not a single action of both types. In (3), the phrase "in itself" indicates the relevance of act-types. A partial paraphrase might run: "Insofar as Sam's action was of the type 'praising Sue,' it was morally neutral," and this clearly leaves open the possibility that the very same action was also of some other type, and as such was *not* morally neutral. Finally, the relation of generation, expressed in (7) with the word "by," may be construed as a complicated relation between actions and their (possibly numerous) types. "Sam made Sue happy by praising her" will on the moderate theory still be thought of as expressing a relation between two actions, one which was of the type "praising Sue" and was a part of the other. The other, larger action was of the type "making her happy." But "Sam praised her by saying 'Very good!'" will be thought of as a relation between an action and two of the (possibly numerous) types it exemplifies. Thus: Sam performed an action of the type "saying 'Very good!'" and because of further circumstances, this action was also of the type "praising Sue."

DISSATISFACTIONS The moderate theory still allows too much proliferation for the taste of some. Can we really add an action of praising Sue together with the resulting change in Sue and say the combination is itself an action, an action of making Sue happy? Actions are events; but this pair seems to remain a pair of events, not a single larger event. If we add the events in between—the impact of Sam's voice on Sue's eardrums, the neural events involved in her hearing and understanding what he said, and so on, the result may be a *process*, rather than something we can call an event in its own right.

What is particularly bothersome is the fact that the change in Sue is allegedly a part of Sam's action, yet it does not take place in Sam at all. Suppose the change took a long time to occur. Better, consider a different example: Sam is in the kitchen preparing to ice a cake, to which end he puts some pieces of chocolate in a pot and puts the pot on a fire. He is "melting the chocolate." According to the moderate theory, this action consists in his putting the pot on the fire (and perhaps also his prior putting the chocolate in the pot) and the change in the chocolate as it melts. But this change takes time, during which Sam may turn to other things entirely. He may even have a heart attack and die! Shall we say that his action is still being performed after his death? Is it not more reasonable to say that his action ended when he put the pot on the fire, but that *consequences* of his action are still occurring?[8]

Finally, the reconstrual of generation from the point of view of the moderate theory is too ungainly. Given only that an agent did an A by doing a B, we must say this is either a relation between one action and two types it exemplified, *or* a relation between two actions and two types they respectively exemplified. But the word "by" seems to have a single sense in all sentences of this form—that is, generation seems to be *one* relation, not a disjunction of two.

THE AUSTERE THEORY   These sources of dissatisfaction and others lead to what we will call the *austere theory of individuation;* according to this theory, if an agent does an A by doing a B, his doing an A and his doing a B are in all cases the same action. A and B are simply two different types this one action exemplified, and the force of the word "by"—the force of saying that his doing a B generated his doing an A—is that the action was of the type A *because* it was of the type B and certain further circumstances obtained. This "because" is asymmetric; we cannot say that Sam's action was of the type "putting the pot on the fire" because it was of the type "melting the chocolate" and certain further circumstances. What made it of the type "melting the chocolate" already includes the circumstances that made it of the type "putting the pot on the fire."[9]

An implication of the austere theory is that actions are confined to the

---

[8] This example is adapted from Thomson, "The Time of a Killing." Cf. the example of Lincoln's assassination mentioned in the Introduction. Similar problems arise regarding the *place* of an action. Beardsley, "Actions and Events," quotes John Dewey as maintaining that if a person in New York kills another in California by sending poisoned candy, "the locus of the act now extends all the way from New York to California." (John Dewey, *Experience and Nature* [New York: Dover Publications, Inc., 1958], p. 198.) But again: is it not more reasonable to say that the *consequences* of the action occur over this distance?

[9] A precise and accurate explanation of the asymmetry is difficult on all the theories considered. See Goldman, *THA*, pp. 38–44; and compare Roderick M. Chisholm, "The Agent as Cause," in Myles Brand and Douglas Walton, eds., *Action Theory* (Dordrecht: D. Reidel Publishing Company, 1976), pp. 199–211.

space occupied by their agents and occur only during such time as their agents are actually doing something. Even Sam's putting the pot on the fire extends no further than his fingertips, because he put the pot on the fire *by* closing his fingers around its handle, moving his arm so the pot was carried to a spot on the fire, then releasing his grasp. His putting the pot on the fire was identical with this sequence of actions; the motion of the pot was no part of them or it. Similarly, the impact of Sam's voice on Sue and the subsequent change in her mood were consequences of his action, not parts of it.[10]

But now the austere theory runs up against the arguments implicit in our statements (4) and (5). The austere theory would have us say that Sam's making Sue happy was identical with his praising her; but the latter *preceded* and *caused* the change in Sue. Can we say, as we would have to on the austere theory, that Sam's making Sue happy preceded and caused her becoming happy?

The evidence allegedly showing that we cannot say these things is the oddity of sentences like:

(9) Sam made Sue happy and then she became happy.

But the oddity can have an explanation other than the one taken for granted by proponents of the prolific and moderate theories. Suppose we assume that the austere theory is correct. Then to say Sam made Sue happy is to say that Sam performed some action which had as an effect that Sue became happy. A correct paraphrase of (9) might then run

(9′) Sam did something which had as an effect that Sue became happy, and then she became happy.

This paraphrase explicitly separates Sam's action from the change in Sue, and it still sounds odd. It sounds odd because the event of Sue's becoming happy is mentioned twice. This is needlessly redundant, and the wording creates the impression that Sue's becoming happy occurred after itself (and not just after the action of Sam's which caused it), which is absurd.

If we accept this explanation of the oddity of (9), we need not regard (4) as true. The evidence for (5) can be disposed of in similar fashion, leaving (6) and parallel examples as the only obstacle confronting the austere theory.

[10] The austere theory has been defended by Donald Davidson in a number of important papers, including "Actions, Reasons, and Causes," *Journal of Philosophy*, LX (1963), pp. 685–700; "The Logical Form of Action Sentences," in Nicholas Rescher, ed., *The Logic of Decision and Action* (Pittsburgh: University of Pittsburgh Press, 1967), pp. 81–95; and "Agency," in Robert Binkley, Richard Bronaugh, and Ausonio Marras, eds., *Agent, Action, and Reason* (Toronto: University of Toronto Press, 1971), pp. 3–25.

According to (6), Sam's praising Sue had the property of "being done in English," but his making her happy did not have this property. A proponent of the austere theory might simply deny the latter half of this claim. His making her happy *was* an action done in English; though if all one knows about the action is that it was of the type "making her happy," one cannot tell that it had this property or was in any way linguistic. This response is less plausible in other examples. Suppose Sam melted the chocolate rapidly—it was a hot fire—but did not put the pot on the fire rapidly. It seems that his melting the chocolate had the property of "being rapid," but his putting the pot on the fire lacked this, and so they cannot be the same action. One response would be to deny that the action was rapid; only the change in the chocolate was. Another would be to say that adverbial modifiers like "rapidly" cannot automatically be regarded as expressing simple properties of events and actions such as "being rapid" is supposed to be. Perhaps the phrase "being rapid" does not specify the property fully enough; we should distinguish "being rapid *as* an action of melting the chocolate," "being rapid *as* an action of putting the pot on the fire," and so on. Perhaps "being rapid" is not a genuine property at all, and we should say only that "melting the chocolate" and "melting the chocolate rapidly" are two closely related types of action, both of which were exemplified by Sam's action.

The proper interpretation of adverbial modifiers is a complex and controversial question.[11] One way or another, though, it seems that this final obstacle confronting the austere theory of individuation can be surmounted.

VOLITIONS   We began this chapter asking about the relation
AND ACTIONS   of Sam's volition to the sound he produced and
                       his action of saying "Very good!" but have so far
said nothing about volitions. It is time to do so.

Many have assumed that volitions are supposed to precede and cause actions. Taking bodily movements like moving one's arm as paradigms, they assume that an action of moving one's arm is identical with the motion of the arm on that occasion. Since the volition is supposed to have caused the latter, it is supposed to have caused the former.

These assumptions, coupled with a conception of volitions as *sui generis* and somewhat mysterious mental phenomena, invited an objection challenging the whole idea that the nature of action is to be explained in terms of volitions.[12] For volitional theories seemed to say

---

11 See, for example, John Wallace, "Some Logical Roles of Adverbs," *Journal of Philosophy*, LXVIII (1971), 690–714; Romane Clark, "Concerning the Logic of Predicate Modifiers," *Nous*, IV (1970), 311–36; and Terence Parsons, "The Logic of Grammatical Modifiers," *Synthese*, XXI (1970), 320–34.

that an action such as moving one's arm qualified as an action because the arm's motion was caused by a volition. Why this genesis should qualify it for that status seemed inexplicable, unless it was assumed that volitions were themselves actions: it was accepted as plausible that a limb motion caused by an action would itself be an action. But then the question arose, what made a volition qualify as an action; and it seemed volitional theories allowed no answer other than causation by *another* volition. In this way, volitional theories of the nature of action were made to appear ridiculous, as requiring an infinite regress of volitions preceding any bodily movement which counted as an action.

This objection in a number of versions was for a number of years widely regarded as conclusively showing the uselessness of the concept of volitions. But more recently it has been answered in many different ways and is now of historical interest only.[13] From the point of view of the volitional theory as developed in the preceding chapter, we should note first that volitions are no more mysterious than any other mental phenomenon, and they may be understood in terms of the functional characterization given. If volitions are themselves actions—as we shall suggest they are—their status as such derives from their "functional connections" with desires and other antecedents of action, with the limb motions and other bodily events they cause, and perhaps most of all with the beliefs to which they contribute, beliefs which constitute awareness of *acting*. As for the concerns of this chapter, however, the crucial point is that on no theory of individuation can the bare motion of a limb *be* an action of moving that limb, because *the action begins with the volition*, not with the limb motion caused by the volition.

The surface evidence for this is the oddity of saying "Sam willed to move his arm and then moved it." Now "willing" is something of a technical term, but volitions are attempts, and "Sam tried to move his arm and then moved it" is entirely nontechnical and sounds just as odd if it is applied to a case in which Sam did not make several attempts before succeeding. Nor can the oddity be explained away; we must conclude that the volition does not precede—and so cannot cause—the action. By contrast, notice that there is no such oddity in "Sam willed to move his arm and then it moved" or in "Sam tried to move his arm and then it moved."

Additional support comes when it is appreciated that generation is not exclusively a relation of actions and act-types. "Sam became president by being elected unanimously" and "Sam got himself excused from jury

12 See Gilbert Ryle, *The Concept of Mind* (New York: Barnes and Noble, Inc., 1949), p. 67. Among the many who repeated Ryle's objection is A. I. Melden, *Free Action* (New York: Humanities Press, Inc., 1961), p. 45.
13 See the authors writing since 1949 listed in the Bibliography to Chapter 1 on versions of the volitional theory.

duty by catching pneumonia" seem to be perfectly acceptable examples of noncausal and causal generation, respectively, though presumably none of the doings involved were actions. Now volitions are attempts, and attempts are doings. They can generate other doings, then—and in particular, it seems that *every doing which is an action is generated by a volition*. Sam made Sue happy by praising her, which he did by saying "Very good!" which he did by willing or by trying to do so. Precisely what it means to say that a particular doing was an action, according to the volitional theory, is that it was generated by a volition. But if generated by a volition, then neither preceded nor caused by a volition.

The temptation to think that the motion of an arm could just by itself *be* someone's action of moving it is of course abetted by the fact that it is an event occurring to a part of the agent's body. This is one reason we have used Sam's saying "Very good!" rather than his moving his arm as our prime example in this chapter. It cannot be very plausible to regard the sound produced by Sam as being, just by itself, this action of his; but why not, if an arm motion can be an action of moving an arm? The answer is that *neither* by itself can be an action; we must not neglect the volition.[14]

If an agent's doing an A was an action, it was generated by a volition. If we accept the prolific theory of individuation, action and volition remain distinct, since they exemplify different types. The volition, for example, may be of the type "willing to say 'Very good!' " and the action generated may be of the type "saying 'Very good! ' "—it is important to note that these are different. Even though distinct, it remains true that the volition does not precede the action, but they begin simultaneously.

If we accept the moderate theory, every action begins with a volition and includes the volition as a part. In every example considered so far, there must also be a doing-related event caused by the volition which is also a part of the action. Thus Sam's praising Sue was identical on this theory with his saying "Very good!" and so included the sound he produced as a part. If there can be an action generated by a volition in a way not involving *causal* generation, then on this theory the action would simply be identical with the volition. Since volitions are mental events, "mental actions" such as someone's effortlessly recalling a name or imagining a horse are the likeliest candidates for such actions. It may not be possible in these cases to draw a line between the willing and the coming-to-consciousness of the name or the image of the horse.[15]

---

14 But see footnote 4 above for references to philosophers who reject this claim.
15 See Hugh McCann, "Volition and Basic Action," *Philosophical Review*, LXXXIII (1974), 451–73, especially 463–66. I suspect, however, that the line *can* be drawn even here. Further study of this problem would benefit from examining Richard Taylor's

Finally, if we accept the austere theory of individuation, we will say that where the agent's doing an A is an action, his doing an A simply *is* the volition which generates it. If Sam's saying "Very good!" was generated by his willing to say "Very good!" then this action was identical with this volition. The distinction between an action and a volition lies simply in the way we conceive it or describe it; there is but one reality.

This conclusion means that actions are mental events, not observable in the straightforward way we generally think. But this may not be an undesirable conclusion. Actions are after all bound up with the psychology of agents; and if we recall the functional characterization of volitions, we will see that the connection with publicly observable events has not really been lost. It is no accident that volitions to move one's arm normally cause motion of one's arm. Moreover, often when we want an explanation of an action, all we are really after is an explanation of why the attempt was made—that is, why the volition occurred. And when we ask if a certain action was "free," or if its agent exercised "free will" in doing it, the crucial issues have to do with the occurrence of the volition. Subsequent events are only of secondary importance. Identifying actions with volitions helps us focus on this.[16]

A conclusive argument in favor of any of the theories and doctrines surveyed in this chapter remains elusive. Perhaps no position on these matters is "the" correct one. In practice, it seems that whatever is said in terms of one theory can be restated in terms of any one of its rivals; a case in point is our reconstrual of Goldman's notion of generation from the viewpoints of the moderate and austere theories.

But one cannot always say things neutrally, in terms of *no* particular one of these theories. For the reasons given above, then, we shall pick the austere theory and henceforth regard actions as identical with volitions. As Prichard maintained (see footnote 16), "to act is really to will something."

---

discussion of "Mental Acts" in his *Action and Purpose* (Englewood Cliffs, N.J.: Prentice-Hall, Inc., 1966), pp. 153–66. Also relevant are Brian O'Shaughnessy, "The Limits of the Will," *Philosophical Review*, LXV (1956), 443–90, and the literature on believing as an action. For the latter, see Arthur C. Danto, *Analytical Philosophy of Action*, pp. 146–50, 192, 217, and 220.

16 What if a volition, say, to move one's arm fails to cause motion of the arm or any other relevant event? Even then we should say that an action has occurred. H. A. Prichard, who held that "to act is really to will something," admitted that "in such cases our activity would not ordinarily be called an action." But he added that the volition is still "of the same sort as what we ordinarily call and think of as an action." ("Action, Willing, Desiring," in his *Moral Obligation* [Oxford: The Clarendon Press, 1949], pp. 187–98; reprinted in Myles Brand, ed., *The Nature of Human Action* [Glenview, Ill.: Scott, Foresman and Company, 1970], pp. 41–49; by permission of the Oxford University Press). His point seems to be adequate enough reason to call it an action even though we "ordinarily" would not.

CHAPTER THREE

Ability

On learning how Sue had avoided a traffic accident, Sam praised her. Could he have done something else instead? We naturally think so. At the precise moment he uttered the words "Very good!" to her, he had the ability to do any number of other things both relevant and irrelevant to the news he had just been given. He could have berated her for driving with an expired license. He could simply have stood there, maintaining silence. He could have started walking away. He could have jumped in the air, or turned a somersault.

There are skeptics about ability who would insist this is all illusion. They believe that fate, or the "laws of nature," or both, lead us in ways unknown to us in detail, but inexorable nonetheless, and no one *can* ever do anything other than what he *does* do. We see how Sam in fact responded to Sue. We may infer, say these skeptics, that nothing else was "really" a possible response for Sam at that moment. If it seems otherwise to us, this is just because our knowledge of the situation, and perhaps of human psychology, is incomplete.

One source of this skepticism is the view called "determinism"; and one direction in which it leads is the denial of what is called "free will."

Both will be examined more closely in later chapters. But on the surface, it seems the skeptics must be wrong. Even if determinism is true, there is an undeniable contrast between these things we say Sam had the ability to do (though he did not do any of them) and others for which he lacked the ability. He could not, for example, have praised Sue in French, not knowing the language. He could not have driven off in his Rolls-Royce, not in fact owning one. And though he could have turned a somersault successfully, he lacked the ability to stand on his head. It ought to be possible to explain this contrast without getting enmeshed in a discussion of free will, and that is what we shall aim at in this chapter.

ABILITY,   The crucial move is to distinguish between ability
POSSIBILITY,   and possibility. We allow the would-be skeptic to
AND LUCK   say it is not possible, in the circumstances that ob-
                                              tain, for a person to do other than he does do;
but this assertion is compatible, we insist, with his having the ability to do otherwise. Confusion arises because the words "can" and "could" are used for both ability and possibility. But Sam "could" have turned a somersault even if in another sense he "could not" have. This means simply that at the time in question, he had the ability to turn a somersault, even if at that time it was not possible for him to exercise this ability.

Nor is this a merely verbal maneuver. Suppose Sam and his three-month-old baby brother are sound asleep. It is not possible for either one to turn a somersault, yet Sam has the ability to turn one and his brother does not. This is a real difference between them. For that matter, it is "possible" that Sam's brother, when awake, puts his head to the floor and tumbles over in a somersault, though he lacks the ability. His success would be entirely a matter of *luck*.

What is the difference between doing something by exercising one's ability to do it, and doing it as a matter of luck? In the most straightforward cases, the answer is, "a reliable connection between attempt and success." Unlike his brother, Sam is entitled to be confident, as he puts his head to the floor, that he will turn over smoothly. If, however, he tries to stand on his head, he is not entitled to similar confidence. On occasion he might succeed, but this would be mere luck. As he lifted his feet off the ground, Sam would have no reason for expecting to attain and retain the inverted position. He has not yet acquired the ability.

The "reliable connection" that is needed may be formulated as a conditional: "If the agent tries to perform an action of the type in question, he will succeed." Or since the time in which we are interested may be past, and the agent may not have exercised his ability, we should use the subjunctive mood. As a first approximation, "At time t the agent x had the ability to do an A" means:

(1) At t, if x had tried to do an A, he would have done an A (thereby).

A number of refinements will prove necessary, but at the heart of all statements attributing an ability to an agent is the assertion of a reliable connection of this sort. Since a subjunctive conditional beginning with the word "if" is relevant to explaining this connection, statements of ability are "constitutionally iffy," in J. L. Austin's phrase.[1]

**DEVELOPING
A CONDITIONAL
ANALYSIS**
The centrality of a subjunctive conditional in the analysis of statements of ability was recognized by G. E. Moore in 1912. Against the skeptical view that nobody could do other than he in fact did, Moore asserted that he "could have walked a mile in twenty minutes this morning" though he in fact did not. And he suggested that what was meant by this assertion was that "I *should, if* I had chosen."[2] More fully:

(2) That morning, if Moore had chosen to walk a mile in twenty minutes, he would (successfully) have walked a mile in twenty minutes.

He did not choose to walk that mile, and so he did not in fact walk it; but he had the ability, he *could* have walked it. On the other hand, he did not have the ability then to run two miles in five minutes. Even if he had chosen to do so, he would not have succeeded.

Moore's proposal (2) is a subjunctive conditional like (1), differing mainly in substituting "chosen" for "tried." Others have favored "wanted," "decided," or some combination of these and others.[3] Now a feature of these alternatives to "tried" is that they all have to do with *antecedents* of action. The choice, decision, desire, or whatever is thought to be an event or state which occurs or obtains before (even if *just* before) the action chosen, decided upon, wanted, or whatever. "Try-

---

[1] J. L. Austin, "Ifs and Cans," *Proceedings of the British Academy*, XLII (Oxford: Oxford University Press, 1956); reprinted in Myles Brand, ed., *The Nature of Human Action* (Glenview, Ill.: Scott, Foresman and Company, 1970), pp. 161–78 (hereafter referred to as *NHA*). Austin himself argued that statements of ability are *not* "constitutionally iffy."

[2] G. E. Moore, *Ethics* (Oxford: The Clarendon Press, 1912), chap. 6; reprinted in Brand, *NHA*, pp. 148–60; by permission of the Oxford University Press. The quoted passage is on p. 151 in Brand. Moore also suggested "I could, if I had chosen" as a possible analysis; see Austin, "Ifs and Cans," and other articles reprinted in Brand for discussion of Moore's proposals.

[3] An excellent example is Alvin I. Goldman, *A Theory of Human Action* (Englewood Cliffs, N.J.: Prentice-Hall, Inc., 1970; Princeton Paperback, 1976), pp. 197–207; see also pp. 63–67. (Hereafter referred to as *THA*.)

ing" differs: it is the action itself, not something which precedes. Actions are volitions, and volitions are attempts. A successful attempt to walk a mile in twenty minutes is just an appropriate set of volitions occurring over a twenty-minute period which cause the legs and hence the whole person to traverse the distance. A successful attempt to turn a somersault is just an appropriate volition (or set of volitions, but for simplicity we will consider them as one) which does result in the body's turning over appropriately.

There is a reason for preferring (1) to alternatives like (2) which refer to antecedents of action: an action of a given type might occur without any of these antecedents. Not every action is chosen, decided upon, wanted, or anything similar. Every action is a volition, and a volition to do an A was characterized as "likely to occur when the agent wants or has other reason to do an A." This was a deliberately vague formulation, allowing for all the possible antecedents of an attempt to do an A and also allowing for the possibility that a volition to do an A—hence a successful action of type A—might occur even if the agent neither wanted nor had any other reason to do an A.

Why is this a reason for preferring (1)? Imagine that at a certain moment Sam had the ability to turn a somersault, but had an audience and was very self-conscious. If at *t* he had made some sort of conscious decision or choice to turn a somersault, or if he was aware that this was indeed what he wanted to do, he would have been so nervous that he would have failed. Yet if at *t* he had simply *done* it spontaneously, without any preliminary—if at *t* the appropriate volition had simply *occurred* —there would have been no impediment, external or internal, and he would have turned a flawless somersault.

In this imaginary situation, subjunctive conditionals employing alternatives to "tried" are all false. It is not true, for example, that "at *t*, if Sam had chosen to turn a somersault, he would have turned a somersault." But it is supposed to be true that at *t*, he did have the ability to turn one. None of these subjunctive conditionals, then, can be a correct analysis of the ability statement. On the other hand, a subjunctive conditional patterned after (1) *is* true: "At *t*, if Sam had tried to turn a somersault, he would have turned one (thereby)." For examples like this, then, (1) seems to provide an adequate analysis.

But not even (1) will serve for a general analysis covering all cases. The reason is similar. Just as not every action of type A is preceded by a choice or desire to do an A, so not every action of type A can be called a successful attempt to do an A. One reason is that the agent may have been trying to do something else; his doing an A may have been generated by his trying to do a B. Now imagine an apparently poor marksman who consistently hits a spot to the left of the spot he aims at. Using (1), we would conclude that he lacks the ability to hit the bull's-eye, since "At t, if he had tried to hit the bull's-eye, he would have done so (thereby)" is false. But it seems he does have the ability to hit the bull's-eye: all he need do is aim for—try to hit—a spot to the *right* of the bull's-eye!

To accommodate this difficulty, we should leave the act-type which is the object of the trying unspecified. Also, we should switch from the word "trying" to the word "willing." This is because in some contexts, the former word reports an effort or preparatory step taken prior to the action, i.e., an antecedent instead of the action (the volition) itself. Our second approximation to the meaning of "at t, x had the ability to do an A" is then:

(3) There is an act-type B such that at t, if x had willed to do a B, he would have done an A (thereby).

At t, if volitions appropriate for aiming at a spot to the right of the bull's-eye had occurred in the marksman, he would have hit the bull's-eye; so (3) allows us to say he did have the ability.

The need for these changes may be questioned. If at t the marksman had not realized the problem with his performance, then no matter how hard he tried he still would not have hit the bull's-eye. This suggests that he did not have the ability, and that (1) was all right as it stood. We can avoid debate on this point by tolerantly recognizing two senses in which we may say a person "has the ability to do an A" at a time t. In the *epistemic* sense, a person had the ability only if at t he knew what to try to do (or: will to do) in order to do an A. We have been discussing the *nonepistemic* sense. The nonepistemic sense seems more fundamental. A person may have abilities he does not know he has; the marksman may have the ability to hit the bull's-eye, though through ignorance (not inability) he keeps missing. But at times we do employ the epistemic sense. In any case, it is easy enough to formulate an analysis of the epistemic sense given an analysis of the nonepistemic sense. For example, (3) could be revised to read "There is an act-type B such that at t, x knew that if he willed to do a B, he would do an A (thereby)."[4]

We shall consider one further complication in this section. If (3) is our analysis, x has the ability to do an A only if the appropriate volitions would generate the agent's doing an A—that is, without fail. But ability is compatible with occasional failure. J. L. Austin made this point, arguing that a golfer may have the ability to sink short putts, yet miss one on occasion for no discernible reason.[5] We should not say that on such occasions the golfer has "temporarily lost the ability"; we have no reason

---

[4] Goldman, *THA*, p. 203, also discusses epistemic and nonepistemic senses.
[5] Austin, "Ifs and Cans," p. 169 in Brand, *NHA*.

to think so (his hands did not shake, nothing interfered with his vision, etc.). Arnold S. Kaufman agreed: a marksman concerning whose ability we have no question may just happen to miss an important target.[6] Kaufman added, however, that "there are some abilities that seem to require invariable success," of which the ability to move one's finger is an example:

. . . if someone had the opportunity to move his finger, tried, yet failed, we should deny that he had had the ability on that occasion. If we were convinced that he really had tried, we should insist that this was conclusive proof that the finger was, in fact, momentarily paralyzed [depriving him of the ability].

Why, then, Kaufman goes on to ask, "should we admit one criterion of performance in the case of one ability, but another criterion in the case of some other ability?"

For an answer, Kaufman directs our attention to the underlying conditions and mechanisms whose presence explains why an attempt on the part of the agent is as likely as it is to be successful. The condition underlying the marksman's ability is more complex in relevant ways than the condition underlying a normal agent's ability to move his finger. Occasional malfunctioning is more likely the more complex the underlying condition, so we do not regard occasional failure as implying absence of the ability. But moving one's finger is "simple enough" so that if there is any failure at all, we say the person lacks the ability.

It would be hard to spell out the kind of "complexity" Kaufman has in mind, and there may be other factors relevant to a judgment that an agent has a certain ability despite an inexplicable failure or two. We shall proceed as if the task were already accomplished, and revise (3) to:

(4) There is an act-type B such that at t, there was an appropriately high probability that if x had willed to do a B, he would have done an A (thereby).

"Appropriateness" is relative to the act-type A and to other relevant factors in ways we shall not try to specify.[7] Nor shall we try to say how

---

6 Arnold S. Kaufman, "Ability," *Journal of Philosophy*, LX (1963), 537–51; reprinted in Brand, *NHA*, pp. 192–203. The passage quoted below is on p. 194 in Brand.

7 In the classic opening passage of his *Manual*, the Stoic philosopher Epictetus writes as if relative to *every* act-type, the probability must be *one*—that is, complete certainty. For his position is that we lack the ability to affect—i.e., to affect reliably—anything external to our own minds: "Of all existing things, some are in our power, and others are not in our power. In our power are thought, impulse, will to get and will to avoid, and, in a word, everything which is our own doing. Things not in our power include the body, property, reputation, office, and, in a word, everything which is not our own doing." Epictetus goes on to claim that the wise man will limit his concern to things in his power. (Translation by P. E. Matheson, in Whitney J. Oates, ed., *The Stoic and Epicurean Philosophers* [New York: The Modern Library, Inc., 1940; copyright 1940 by Random House, Inc.], p. 468).

the "probability" is to be determined. It is hoped that these gaps in our analysis will not matter.

AN OBJECTION
TO CONDITIONAL
ANALYSES

Another difficulty in (4) very definitely does matter. Despite all the changes, (4) is still essentially a subjunctive conditional, like (1). It says that *if* a certain condition had been met, then something else would (probably) have been the case. Disregarding the word "probably," it says that *if* a volition with the right object had occurred in *x* at *t,* then *x* would have done an A. There is an obvious question: *could* a volition with that object have occurred at *t?* And if not, can we really say that *x* had the ability to do an A?

The question could have been raised about (1), though we carefully avoided doing so. Sam, we said, had the ability to turn a somersault despite his stage fright, because *if* he had gone ahead and "tried" to turn one, he would have turned one. But was he *able to try* at that moment? Could the appropriate volition have occurred?

Since the time of Moore's proposals, advocates of conditional analyses of ability statements like (1) and (4) have struggled with this question. Opponents have found in it evidence that statements of ability are *categorical.* Each of these statements implies that at the time in question, something is the case, "categorically," and their meaning cannot be given wholly in terms of subjunctive conditionals, however complicated.[8]

The force of the objection is blunted somewhat by the distinction we drew between ability and possibility. All that follows from Sam's nervousness and the fact that a volition to turn a somersault cannot occur in him when he is so nervous is that he cannot exercise his ability. It does not follow that he does not have the ability.

But the maneuver is too successful. A purely conditional analysis like (4) implies that Sam has a number of other abilities which he in fact may lack.

Consider: can Sam wiggle his ears? We naturally think that some people have this ability and others lack it. Sam is our own creation, so we can imagine him either way. But our discussion so far suggests he had this ability at *t* if the following is true:

(5) At *t,* there was an appropriately high probability that if Sam had willed to wiggle his ears, he would have wiggled them (thereby).

[8] Versions of this objection have been pressed by Roderick M. Chisholm, "J. L. Austin's Philosophical Papers," *Mind,* LXXIII (1964), 20–25, excerpted in Brand, *NHA,* pp. 187–91, and many who take a "libertarian" or "hard determinist" position on free will. (See Chapter 6 and the Bibliography thereto.) Conditional analyses are also opposed by Richard Taylor, *Action and Purpose* (Englewood Cliffs, N.J.: Prentice-Hall, Inc., 1966), chap. 4.

By "willing to wiggle his ears" is not meant anything like "closing one's eyes really tight and imagining one's ears wiggling" or "thinking the command 'Wiggle!' as addressed to one's ears." Rather, a willing to wiggle one's ears is a volition with "wiggling one's ears" as its object. Following the functional characterization of volitions presented in Chapter 1, we can say that such a volition is an event likely to occur when the agent wants or has other reason to wiggle his ears, which normally causes the agent to believe he is wiggling his ears, and normally causes his ears to wiggle. It must also be the case that the likelihood of its occurrence is not affected by beliefs the agent may happen to have about *how* he wiggles his ears; for example, this distinguishes a volition to wiggle one's ears from volitions which would generate the agent's grasping his ears in his hands and shaking them. Events of this sort undoubtedly occur, in people who we agree have the ability to wiggle their ears and who have exercised this ability. But do they occur in *Sam*? It does not matter; (5) does not assert that they do occur or even that they *could* occur. Instead, (5) asserts that *if* such a volition were to occur in Sam, there would be an "appropriately high probability" that it would generate Sam's wiggling his ears. And this seems to be true. For a volition with this object "normally" causes the agent's ears to wiggle. Whatever "normally" means, it seems safe to infer that there would be an "appropriately high probability" of success. But then (5) is true, and our analysis implies that Sam has the ability to wiggle his ears.

Something is radically wrong.

Imagine now that in fact Sam does not have the ability to wiggle his ears. The relevant facial muscles are there, in good enough working order. It is just that volitions which would cause them to contract never occur, indeed *cannot occur* in Sam no matter how much he "wants or has other reason" to wiggle them, unless and until he learns how to wiggle them. Now we also imagined that volitions which would cause Sam's body to turn over in a somersault cannot occur when Sam has an audience. But there is a difference. Sam has already learned how to turn somersaults; appropriate volitions have occurred in him in the past, and he has not forgotten what he has learned. Rather, it is stage fright that prevents their occurrence when other people are present. We will say that "turning a somersault" is *in his repertoire* but "wiggling one's ears" is not in his repertoire. (For simplicity, we are assuming that when Sam turns a somersault, the act-type "turning a somersault" is the object of his volition.)

Suppose we build a reference to this "repertoire" into our analysis of statements of ability. Instead of (4) we now have:

(6) There is an act-type B such that at *t*, B was in *x*'s repertoire, and there was

an appropriately high probability that if x had willed to do a B, he would have done an A (thereby).

Since "wiggling one's ears" was not in Sam's repertoire at t, our analysis no longer implies that Sam had the ability to wiggle his ears. On the other hand:

(7) At t, "turning a somersault" was in Sam's repertoire, and there was an appropriately high probability that if Sam had willed to turn a somersault, he would have done so (thereby).

is true, even though his stage fright made it impossible for a volition with this object to occur at t. Our analysis preserves the implication we want, that Sam did have the ability to turn a somersault, even though it could not be exercised at that time.

But what does it mean to say that a certain act-type was in the agent's repertoire at a certain time?

REPERTOIRES

An act-type A is in an agent's repertoire at t if by t he has "learned how" to do an A by willing to do an A. (Wiggling one's ears by grasping them in one's hands and shaking them is not wiggling them by willing to wiggle them.) This explanation does not help much, because "learning how" just means "acquiring the ability," the very idea we are trying to understand. Nor will it help to say A is in his repertoire if volitions to do an A "can occur" in him, for as we have just seen, A may be in his repertoire at t even if volitions to do an A cannot occur in him at t. What we want is a special sense in which the volitions can occur in a person who has learned how, even if in another sense they cannot occur.

We understand volitions as functionally characterized events, and we have mentioned the view that all mental events and states may be so understood. This approach invites comparisons between persons and computers, because the events and states involved when a computer does something it has been programmed to do may also be understood in this way.[9] A comparison of this sort may help us here.

Asking Sam to wiggle his ears or to turn a somersault is like asking a computer to print out the square root of 25. Whether the computer does so depends only partly on whether the computer is physically equipped to print the numeral "5." It also matters how the computer is programmed and what else it is doing at the time (or has just been doing).

---

[9] For literature developing and making use of these comparisons, see the Bibliography to Chapter 1 on the "functionalist" view of mental events and states, especially the papers by Putnam, and Harman's book.

For example, it may never have been "set" to respond correctly to any instructions about square roots. Perhaps its "5"-printing mechanism operates only when it is asked to compute sums like $2 + 3$, or $44 + 11$. Perhaps it has been programmed in such a way that *no* instructions it is likely to be given will lead to the operation of this particular mechanism. This last state of affairs corresponds to that of Sam insofar as wiggling his ears is concerned. The muscles are there, but neither being asked to wiggle his ears nor being in any other likely situation will lead to contraction of those muscles. "Wiggling one's ears" is not in his repertoire. Alternatively, the computer may have been programmed to handle instructions about square roots, but also to disregard such instructions under certain conditions. This corresponds to Sam insofar as turning a somersault is concerned. The requisite "circuitry" has been set up; it is *possible* that when Sam has been asked, wants, or has other reason to turn a somersault, a volition to turn one will ensue. Sam's psychology is such, however, that under certain conditions—specifically, when he is aware of having an audience—the "instruction to turn a somersault" will be disregarded. This is the sense in which it is *not* possible that a volition to turn a somersault will occur at these times. Still, the circuitry is there, the computing system which is Sam has been programmed for turning somersaults. "Turning a somersault" is in his repertoire, and he has the ability to turn one even at times when he cannot exercise this ability.

A few additional points about repertoires may be noted before we return to the topic of ability.

The set of act-types in one's repertoire at a given time are the things one can *will* to do, not necessarily the things one can actually *do,* successfully. A person with a paralyzed arm lacks the ability to move the arm (by willing to move it; let us ignore the fact that he can move it, e.g., by lifting it with the other arm). Still, "moving the arm" remains in his repertoire. This is shown by the fact that if his doctor asks him to "try to move it," he is likely to respond by willing to move it. In this sense, he has not forgotten how to move the arm.[10]

---

[10] Goldman, *THA,* p. 67, speaks of "moving one's arm" being a *basic act-type* for a given agent at a given time. His notion corresponds closely to our saying it is in the agent's repertoire at that time, with the important difference that it is *not* a basic act-type for the agent if the agent is paralyzed or otherwise prevented from succeeding if he wills to move his arm. Other writers have used related concepts of "basic actions." The terms "repertoire" and "basic action" were both introduced by Arthur C. Danto in two important and stimulating papers: "What We Can Do," *Journal of Philosophy,* LX (1963), 435–45; and "Basic Actions," *American Philosophical Quarterly,* 2 (1965), 141–48. The latter is reprinted in Brand, *NHA,* pp. 255–66. Both are reprinted in Norman S. Care and Charles Landesman, eds. *Readings in the Theory of Action* (Bloomington: Indiana University Press, 1968), pp. 113–26 and 93–112, respectively. See also Danto's later discussion in his *Analytical Philosophy of Action* (Cambridge: Cambridge University Press, 1973).

Some authors have argued in effect that what one wills—the act-types in one's repertoire—must always be the bringing about of a change in one's own body, as when one wills to move an arm. More cautiously, it is allowed that mental act-types like "imagining a horse" or "calculating mentally the sum of 16 and 9" may be exceptions. But even with these exceptions the claim is incorrect, if our functional characterization of a "volition to do an A" is accepted. For we stipulated that a volition to do an A is an event whose likelihood of occurrence is independent of any beliefs the agent may happen to have about how he does or can do an A. This stipulation is certainly met in the case of volitions to move particular parts of the body. Whether or not an appropriate volition occurs in Sam when he is asked to move his arm or to turn a somersault, has nothing to do with his physiological knowledge of the muscles or neurons whose activity is required. But the stipulation is also met in the case of volitions whose objects are linguistic act-types. Sam's saying "Very good!" to Sue may have been generated, for example, by a single volition with the object "saying 'Very good!' " Occurrence of this volition is independent of any beliefs Sam may have had about *how* he says "Very good!"— beyond general awareness that his lips, tongue, and vocal cords are involved he probably does not have any such beliefs!

Finally, there are other act-types which may be in an agent's repertoire though successful actions of these types involve production of specific effects in objects beyond the agent's body—"tying one's shoes," for example. True, one ties one's shoes by moving hands and fingers in certain intricate ways; but experienced agents do not have to think how to move them. They "simply" tie their shoes. It follows that such beliefs as they may have about how they tie their shoes do not play any role in their performance, and so the stipulation is met for the volition involved to have "tying one's shoes" as its object. "Typing the letter 'S' " and perhaps even "stopping the car" are examples of other act-types involving effects beyond the agent which may be in the repertoires of some agents.[11]

One of the most interesting features of repertoires is implicit in the preceding: though most of us have many of the same act-types in our repertoires, our repertoires do differ, and even the repertoire of a single agent may change over time. Infants do acquire the ability to turn somersaults, and this involves an addition to their repertoires as much as it involves maturation of their skeletal muscles. Sam can learn how to wiggle his ears, and techniques of biofeedback have allegedly enabled people

[11] For more on what can and cannot be in an agent's repertoire, see the references mentioned in footnote 15 of Chapter 2, the Bibliography to Chapter 4 on "negative events" and "negative actions," the final section of Chapter 4, and the Bibliography to this chapter. My review of Danto's book in *Journal of Philosophy*, LXXIII (1976), 99–107, explores Danto's suggestion that a person's "body" extends *by definition* as far as the things with which he can perform basic actions.

to add such act-types as "lowering one's heart rate" to their repertoires. Learning to speak a new language also involves expansion of one's repertoire, assuming one progresses beyond the need to translate from one's native language with the help of memorized vocabulary lists and set patterns for sentence construction. Loss to one's repertoire is less common; remember that paralysis deprives one of the ability but does not diminish one's repertoire. Perhaps aphasia caused by brain damage supplies examples. A person so afflicted may have lost the ability, say, to utter the word "pencil" when-shown a pencil and asked to say what it is. What has gone wrong may be more than loss of the "reliable connection between attempt and success" required for ability. Rather, the very circuitry needed if there is to be such an attempt may be gone; the person's repertoire has suffered loss of the act-type "saying the word 'pencil.' "[12]

ABILITY NOW TO ACT LATER The analysis of "At t, x had the ability to do an A" at which we have arrived is:

(6) There is an act-type B such that at t, B was in x's repertoire, and there was an appropriately high probability that if x had willed to do a B, he would have done an A (thereby).

This is most naturally read as if the phrase "at t" were explicitly mentioned as the time of the volition's occurrence and the time of the agent's doing an A. If at t Sam willed to wiggle his ears, if the volition caused his ears to wiggle, and if its doing so could not be attributed to luck, then he wiggled his ears at t, and it is true to say that at t he had the ability to wiggle his ears at t. For many types of actions in many situations, this analysis presents no problems. For these cases, (6) seems at last to be entirely adequate. (Notice, however, that with the addition of a reference to the agent's repertoire, it is no longer a purely conditional analysis. The subjunctive conditional is only part of (6).)

But actions of many types are not generated by a single volition occurring at the same time the agent is said to have the ability. For convenience we treated "turning a somersault" as if only a single volition were involved, and this may be so. But it is also possible that turning a somersault is best viewed as involving several volitions with distinct objects, occurring simultaneously or over a brief interval of time. Our treatment of the marksman example was almost certainly defective in this respect. Rather than a single volition with the object "shooting at a spot to the right of the bull's-eye," we should have in mind two volitions occurring in succession, whose objects are "aiming at a spot to the right

---

12 On the subject of changes in repertoires, see Danto, *Analytical Philosophy of Action*, chap. 5.

of the bull's-eye" and "shooting" (or "pulling the trigger"). The time elapsing between the volitions may be brief, but strictly the agent does an A not "at t" but *by* some later time, t'. And the interval from t to t' may be long. Roderick Chisholm offers the example of an agent who today (t) has the ability to travel to Boston tomorrow (t'). This agent can buy a ticket today, and only if he does so will his stepping on the train tomorrow lead to his arriving in Boston later in the day (rather than his being thrown off at some intermediate point).[13]

To handle all these kinds of cases, we need to consider not "At t, x had the ability to do an A (at t)," but "At t, x had the ability to do an A by t'," where t' may be later than t. And the required analysis will speak not merely of one act-type B and one volition to do a B, but a sequence of volitions with different objects occurring at specified times during the interval from t to t'. There may be flexibility—in the travel-to-Boston case, it does not matter precisely when volitions occur that would generate the agent's buying a ticket, so long as they occur before all the available space is reserved. What the analysis must assert is the existence of at least one set of act-types in the agent's repertoire, and at least one corresponding set of times during the interval, such that if volitions with these act-types as objects occur at these times, the agent will (probably) do or have done an A by t'.

For example, consider:

(8) There is at least one set of act-types $B_1 \ldots B_n$, and at least one set of times $t_1 \ldots t_n$ in the interval from t to t', such that $B_1 \ldots B_n$ were in x's repertoire during the interval, and there was an appropriately high probability that if at t_1 x had willed to do a B_1, at t_2 had willed to do a B_2, $\ldots$, and at t_n had willed to do a B_n, then x would have done an A by t'.

In the travel-to-Boston case, B_1 might be "walking to the door," on the way to the station to buy a ticket. B_n might be "stepping up," onto the relevant train, with the ticket in one's pocket. As mentioned, there may be many choices for the corresponding times, limited only by the need to purchase a ticket early enough, and to get on a train that will indeed arrive in Boston by t'. Notice that two or more of the times may be identical, to cover situations in which the agent must do two or more things simultaneously. And in the limiting case where t and t' are themselves identical, and the set of act-types has only one member, (8) becomes equivalent to (6).

[13] Roderick M. Chisholm, " 'He Could Have Done Otherwise,' " *Journal of Philosophy*, LXIV (1967), 409–17; a revised version is reprinted in Brand, *NHA*, pp. 293–301. The refinements introduced here to accommodate these cases may usefully be compared with Chisholm's suggestions in this paper and in his "The Agent as Cause," in Myles Brand and Douglas Walton, eds., *Action Theory* (Dordrecht: D. Reidel Publishing Company, 1976), pp. 199–211, and with Goldman's suggestions, *THA*, pp. 204–6.

But (8) is too stringent. We have remarked that an agent's repertoire may change over time. There is no need, then, to require all the act-types $B_1 \ldots B_n$ to be in the agent's repertoire throughout the interval from t to t'. It is enough if at each of the moments t_i, the corresponding B_i is in his repertoire. As a fanciful example, suppose that none of the usual means of transportation was available to Sam, but at t a friend offered to drive him to Boston by t' on condition that he wiggle his ears. At t, "wiggling one's ears" may not be in Sam's repertoire. But perhaps there is something he can do starting at t—training using biofeedback, perhaps—as a result of which he will "learn how" to wiggle his ears and do so with enough time remaining for his friend to get him to Boston by t' as promised. If this is so, we must say that at t, Sam does have the ability to get to Boston by t'.

Before trying to revise (8) in the light of this, we must note a respect in which (8) is not stringent enough. We must consider the possibility that a consequence of one of the required volitions may be that a volition required later cannot occur. Suppose the condition set by Sam's friend had been that Sam swallow a sleeping pill and turn a somersault one hour later. Both "swallowing a pill" and "turning a somersault" may be in Sam's repertoire throughout the interval from t to t', so if (8) is our analysis, we would have to say that Sam had the ability at t to get to Boston by t'. But if he takes the pill, say, at t_1, he will be asleep an hour later, and so it will be impossible for a volition to turn a somersault to occur then. It appears, then, that he did *not* have the ability at t to get to Boston by t'.

Assuming this is correct, we need to revise (8) in a fairly complicated way. We must require that the volitions and their consequences will not interfere with each other, that it is *possible* for them all to occur, in order, at the specified times. "At t, x had the ability to do an A by t'" means something on the order of:

(9) There is at least one set of act-types $B_1 \ldots B_n$, and at least one set of times $t_1 \ldots t_n$ in the interval from t to t', such that:

   (i) B_1 was in x's repertoire at t_1;

   (ii) for each i from 1 through $(n-1)$, there was an appropriately high probability that if at t_1 x had willed to do a B_1, at t_2 had willed to do a B_2, . . . , and at t_i had willed to do a B_i, then at t_{i+1}, B_{i+1} would have been in x's repertoire and it would have been possible that at t_{i+1}, x willed to do a B_{i+1}; and

   (iii) if at t_1 x had willed to do a B_1, at t_2 had willed to do a B_2, . . . , and at t_n had willed to do a B_n, then x would have done an A by t'.

The difference between (8) and (9) lies in clause (ii). Notice how it provides both for the requisite act-types to be in the agent's repertoire at the proper times and for volitions with those act-types as objects to be possible at those times.

We have arrived at a position that may seem paradoxical, even inconsistent with claims made earlier. Suppose we specify a time t_1 and another time t_2 one hour later. At t_1, Sam had the ability to swallow a sleeping pill. Suppose he exercised this ability. Still, at t_2 he had the ability to turn a somersault. The fact that he was asleep means only that it was not possible that this ability be exercised at t_2. Ability and possibility of exercising an ability, we have urged, must be carefully distinguished. Now, however, we say that at t_1 he did *not* have the ability to swallow the pill at t_1 and turn a somersault at t_2. And our reason is that exercise of the first ability mentioned (to swallow the pill at t_1) would make exercise of the second ability (to turn a somersault at t_2) impossible. The possibility of exercising an ability seems relevant after all to possession of ability.

There is no actual inconsistency here. Ability and possibility of exercising that ability remain distinct. Ability at t_1 to swallow the pill at t_1 and turn a somersault at t_2 is the third ability under discussion. Sam is said to lack this third ability because exercise of the first would make exercise of the second impossible. If Sam was unaffected by sleeping pills and so at t_1 had this third ability, it would be a separate question whether there was any possibility of his exercising it. (He might have been asleep at t_1!) Notice that (9) does not require that a volition to do a B_1 be "possible" at t_1. It requires only that B_1 be in x's repertoire at t_1, parallel to the requirement in (6) that B be in x's repertoire at t.

Problems remain with (9), including the exact force of the word "possible" and of course the phrase "appropriately high probability." But (9) is clear enough as an analysis of statements of ability to justify discounting the skeptical view mentioned at the beginning of this chapter. Whatever is decided about free will and determinism, we can safely say that what we have the ability to do is not limited to what we actually do.

CHAPTER FOUR

Intention

Actions are volitions; *intentional* actions are . . . what? It is remarkable that we have come so far in discussing action while saying so little in answer to this question, because many have argued or assumed that "action" and "intentional action" are virtually equivalent. Of course an agent may do something unintentionally. In Chapter 2 we mentioned the possibility that Sam made Sue happy unintentionally. But he did it by saying "Very good!" to her, and this he did intentionally. What he did intentionally and what he did unintentionally were not two actions, one intentional and the other unintentional. Rather, we suggested that intention is a matter of "how the agent thought of the action," in particular, what *type* he thought of it as exemplifying. Sam's one action was of more than one type. He did think of it as of the type "saying 'Very good!' " but did not think of it as of the type "making Sue happy." Many writers on action theory suspect that every action is of at least one type such that the agent thought of it as exemplifying that type, and in this sense they believe that every action is intentional.[1] Whether they are right depends

1 For example, Donald Davidson, "Agency," in Robert Binkley, Richard Bronaugh, and Ausonio Marras, eds., *Agent, Action, and Reason* (Toronto: University of Toronto Press, 1971), p. 7.

on how we are to understand the vague phrase "how the agent thought of the action."

Related to this claim that every action is intentional is the claim that we are always acting intentionally, at least while awake. Stuart Hampshire argues:

> . . . at any moment there are a number of things that [a person] can truly be said to intend to do in the future, and also something that he can be truly said to be intentionally doing at the present, provided that he is conscious and therefore active.[2]

George Miller, Eugene Galanter, and Karl Pribram make the same claim in terms of their theoretical notion of a "Plan":

> What does it mean when an ordinary man has an ordinary intention? It means that he has begun the execution of a Plan and that this intended action is a part of it. . . .
> . . . Plans are executed because people are alive. This is not a facetious statement, for so long as people are behaving, *some* Plan or other must be executed.[3]

These writers clearly feel that this claim expresses something fundamental about the kind of creatures we human beings are and about the structure of the lives we lead.

Both these claims make intention of central importance in considering action. A related claim is that when an action is of two types, A and B, such that the agent did an A intentionally and a B unintentionally, the description of him as doing an A is "privileged." Sometimes it is said that the agent "really" only did an A; it is only this that he is accountable for, only this that must be explained in "the" explanation of what he did. (Can Sam properly be praised for making Sue happy if he did not intend this? Can we explain his making Sue happy except by explaining what led him to say "Very good!" to her?) This partly explains why establishing an agent's intentions is of importance to juries and social scientists. Similarly, literary critics and constitutional lawyers often try to identify the intentions of the authors of the documents with which they are concerned.

It can be very difficult to determine an agent's intentions, and so it has been argued in each of these areas that it is unnecessary, even undesirable, to do so. Such arguments may be best assessed if we have a clear understanding of what we are looking for when we inquire into an agent's intentions. In this chapter we will take a step toward such an understanding.

[2] Stuart Hampshire, *Thought and Action* (London: Chatto and Windus, 1960), p. 100.
[3] George A. Miller, Eugene Galanter, and Karl H. Pribram, *Plans and the Structure of Behavior* (New York: Holt, Rinehart and Winston, Inc., 1960), pp. 61–62.

ACTING
INTENTIONALLY
AND INTENDING

If Sam intends to do an A, he has not yet done it. Intending is a state which precedes action. In developing the volitional theory, we saw that an action can occur without any antecedent in the form of the agent's wanting or having other reason to perform the action. It is tempting to think that *intentional* action must however be preceded by a state of intending—and if all action is intentional, it would follow that every action has an antecedent of a special kind after all. This temptation must be resisted.

Let us take a second look at examples used in Chapter 1 to show that action need not be preceded by desire.

(a) Sid visited his aunt because he thought he ought to do so.
(b) Sue stepped on the brake when a child suddenly darted out in the path of the car.
(c) Seth absent-mindedly brushed his teeth.
(d) Sal kicked the door in anger.
(e) Sol tore off the thread he had just noticed hanging from his shirt.

Sid very likely formed the intention to visit his aunt before acting on it, so (a) will not help us here. But in connection with (b), we asked if there was time between Sue's perception of the child and the movement of her foot for a desire to stop the car to enter the picture. If not, there is also no room for an intention to have formed—no interval of time, however brief, in which she intended to do what she had not yet even begun doing. She simply saw the child and responded. There is no definite evidence and nothing clearly to be gained by supposing otherwise. Yet she acted intentionally, and to be sure, she may *say* afterward that stopping the car, stepping on the brake, and avoiding the child are all things she intended. But she did not intend these things before acting. Acting intentionally must be sharply distinguished from intending.

We suggested that Seth had gone to the medicine chest for an aspirin, but took out the toothpaste instead from force of habit. He did not intend to brush his teeth. It may be argued that he did not brush his teeth intentionally, either, so that this example does not help us distinguish intending and acting intentionally. But consider: when he took the toothpaste from the medicine chest, surely it was with the intention of brushing his teeth! This pushes us in the other direction: he *did* intend to brush his teeth before he began brushing, and he brushed intentionally. But now, what about his taking the toothpaste out of the medicine chest? We have no evidence whatsoever for thinking he intended to do *this* before he did it. Yet it would be misleading at best to claim he did not do it intentionally: if he did not take the toothpaste out intentionally, how can we say he took it out with the (further) intention of brushing his teeth? Unless we deny that Seth did anything at all intentionally, we must admit he did something intentionally without intending, before-hand, to do it.

The final two examples are of impulsive actions. Again, it is only prejudice, not evidence, which could lead someone to insist that Sal and Sol "must" have intended in advance to do what they did. Yet it is plausible to claim of each, especially Sol, that he acted intentionally. Just as someone may fail ever to do something he once intended to do, so he may do something intentionally which he never intended to do at all. Our study of "intention" must divide into separate treatments of "acting intentionally" and "intending."

ACTING Three factors have been regarded as important in
INTENTIONALLY explaining what it is to do something intentionally: the agent's *reason* for doing it; his *knowledge* that he was doing it; and the fact that doing it was his *purpose,* what he was "aiming at."

The first is often understood in terms of antecedents of the action, especially desires, beliefs, and combinations of desires and beliefs. Sid believed he ought to visit his aunt. Sue saw the child, i.e., believed it was there. Sol saw the thread and may have had a general desire to keep his shirts looking neat. (Note that this is still not to say that he had a desire to tear off the thread he had just noticed, still less that he formed the intention to do so.) But it is not plausible to say that whenever an agent does an A intentionally, he had a reason of this sort for doing an A and did an A because of this reason. Sol's behavior may not have had this background yet may still have been intentional. Sal may have "needed to let off steam," but this does not seem to have functioned as a reason of the sort we are considering. And Seth had no reason at all for brushing his teeth. Philosophers who have attempted to explain acting intentionally in terms of the agent's reason seem for the most part to have failed to distinguish acting intentionally from doing something intended in advance, or else they did not interpret the agent's "reason for doing it" in terms of antecedents.

Most writers who have clearly distinguished between "acting intentionally" and "intending" have emphasized the second factor, the agent's knowledge of what he is doing, in their accounts of acting intentionally. With the possible exception of Sal, all the agents in (a) through (e) knew what they were doing at the time they did it. Seth brushed absent-mindedly, but even he must have been *aware on some level* of what he was doing. Taking out the toothpaste, squeezing some onto the tooth-brush, and the actual brushing involve too much coordination of hand and eye, not to mention the use of memory in locating paste, brush, and water, for us to say his behavior was totally "unconscious."[4] Even Sal did not "connect" with the door by accident. If she had believed the door was heavy and unyielding enough to seriously hurt her foot, she probably would not have kicked at it despite her anger. This suggests that she also "knew what she was doing."

Saying that acting intentionally is essentially a matter of acting with knowledge of what one is doing provides the most natural interpretation of the claim that intention is a matter of "how the agent thought of the action." We shall explore this approach before coming to the third factor, what the agent was "aiming at."

A person may do an A and know that he is doing an A, yet *not* be doing an A intentionally. This is so whenever the agent finds out while doing an A that he is doing it. Imagine that Sam is emptying a can of water by pouring it out the window. He looks, and realizes that he is watering the flowers below. But he is not watering them intentionally.[5]

Now suppose Sam looked before starting, closed his eyes, and then began pouring the water. He can be perfectly confident that he is watering the flowers, and he has not *found out* that he is watering them. His looking out the window only informed him that the flowers were there. True, this information may be essential. His present knowledge that he is watering them may be an inference from this information, his faith in the stability of the world (e.g., the flowers have not disappeared), and his confidence in his own ability to empty the can out the window even with his eyes closed. But the inference would not be warranted without one more bit of information, unavailable to him while his eyes were still open: that he has *begun to act*.

How does he know that he has begun watering the flowers? "He can feel the motions of his arm and wrist." Perhaps. And feeling these motions would be "finding out" that they were taking place. But then how does he know they are moving in ways likely to get the water out of the can, through the window, and so onto the flowers? It is implausible to suggest he remembers from past experience precisely what it feels like to empty a can of water out a window, and realizes that the motions he now feels are like them. Certainly nothing like this goes on consciously.

---

[4] Irving Thalberg, *Enigmas of Agency* (New York: Humanities Press, Inc., 1972), pp. 171–85, discusses the levels of awareness we must say are involved in the activities of sleepwalkers and similarly "unconscious" agents.

[5] If at the moment that he realizes what he is doing he has the ability to stop the flow of water but *intentionally refrains* from doing so, we may say from that point on that he is intentionally watering the flowers. Intentional omissions are briefly discussed at the end of this chapter. This example was suggested by several given by Jack W. Meiland, *The Nature of Intention* (London: Methuen and Co., Ltd., 1970), pp. 86–87. Throughout this excellent book, Meiland goes into many points of detail which we cannot cover here.

No, whatever contribution these "feelings" may make, we must locate the primary source of Sam's knowledge in the volitions which cause the motions of his arm and wrist. Say, for example, that there are two volitions, one with the object "extending one's arm" and the other with the object "turning one's wrist so as to invert the object in one's hand." As noted in Chapter 1, these volitions contribute directly to Sam's awareness (belief) that he is extending his arm and turning his wrist, and they could give him this awareness even if he could not "feel" their motions. Since he already knows that there is a can of water in his hand and that in front of him is an open window with flowers below, these volitions give him his knowledge that he has begun watering the flowers. He has no need to "find out."

Sam's knowledge is an example of what has been called *knowledge without observation*.[6] Even in normal cases where the agent has his eyes open or otherwise knows what he is doing in part because of what his senses are telling him, the agent's volitions make their direct contribution. We will call an agent's knowledge of what he is doing *nonobservational* so long as present testimony of the senses is not essential to it. The claim that the agent's knowledge of what he is doing is of central importance in acting intentionally must be understood as applying to the agent's nonobservational knowledge. One part of this claim is that an agent did an A intentionally only if he knew nonobservationally that he was doing an A; in other words, that nonobservational knowledge is *necessary* for acting intentionally. This is an attractive view; later, however, we shall find reasons for weakening it. Let us now ask whether nonobservational knowledge is *sufficient* for acting intentionally—whether there is nothing else to the idea of acting intentionally than the idea of knowing nonobservationally what one is doing.

"KNOWINGLY" VERSUS "INTENTIONALLY" Suppose Sam tells us that he did not care that the flowers were getting watered; his intention was merely to empty the can. (He extended his arm, let us say, so the floor would not get wet; still, he insists, it is incorrect to say he watered the flowers intentionally.) He knew before emptying the can that his doing so would generate his watering the flowers, so he did have nonobservational knowledge of the latter; but he was not *aiming at* the flowers' getting watered, watering the flowers was not his *purpose* in acting. He would have emptied the can as he did even if the flowers had not been there. Sam is taking the position that

6 G. E. M. Anscombe, *Intention*, 2nd ed. (Oxford: Basil Blackwell, 1963), pp. 13–15, 49–53.

acting knowingly, even with nonobservational knowledge, is not sufficient for acting intentionally. (Henceforth we will use "knowingly" as if it were equivalent to "with nonobservational knowledge.") The third of the three factors we mentioned cannot be left out.

Another illustration of Sam's position, of greater moral significance, is the case of a doctor who removes the cancerous uterus of a pregnant woman, thereby saving her life but causing the death of the fetus. Some Roman Catholics and others who believe that it is always wrong to "intentionally" kill a healthy human fetus nevertheless believe that this doctor's action may be condoned. Though he knowingly caused the fetus to die, he was not aiming at its death. His ultimate aim was to save the woman; he did aim at removal of the uterus as a means to this end. But death of the fetus was neither an end of his nor a means to any end of his. He would have operated in the same way even if the fetus had not been there; and if the fetus somehow survived, the doctor would not feel that he had been frustrated in his action. Consequently, it is urged, we cannot say that the doctor "intentionally" killed the fetus.[7]

Some oppose this view that an agent can do something knowingly yet not intentionally. Since Sam knew in advance that the flowers would get watered if he emptied the can, he could have been influenced by this knowledge not to do it, had there been some reason not to water the flowers. And the doctor knew that he would be causing the fetus to die if he removed the uterus. Like Sam, he acted not merely *in* awareness of what he was doing, but *despite* this awareness. If the action was of a morally questionable type, as killing a human fetus is widely believed to be, the doctor cannot escape responsibility by claiming he did not do it intentionally.

We must separate the moral issues from the problem of what it is to act intentionally. The distinction exemplified in these examples is genuine enough. Whether it has, or should have, the moral significance claimed for it may be debated and has been. Perhaps it is true that the doctor cannot escape responsibility in the case described, but perhaps all this would show is that people need not do something intentionally in order to be "responsible" for it. It may be enough that they do it knowingly. Perhaps it is true, as others argue, that the doctor's action was

---

[7] In another kind of case, a woman in childbirth can be saved only by crushing the skull of the emerging fetus. Here, the Catholic position is that the doctor does "intentionally" cause the fetus to die—presumably as a means to the end of saving the woman, though "causing the fetus to die" is not the same act-type as "crushing the fetus's skull." For critical discussion of the principle used to distinguish these cases, see H. L. A. Hart, "Intention and Punishment," in his *Punishment and Responsibility* (Oxford: Oxford University Press, 1968), pp. 113–35; and Philippa Foot, "The Problem of Abortion and the Doctrine of the Double Effect," in James Rachels, ed., *Moral Problems,* 2nd ed. (New York: Harper and Row, Publishers, 1971), pp. 59–70.

entirely justified, and would be so even if we agreed that he "intentionally" caused the fetus to die. All this would show is that in some circumstances it is all right to intentionally perform actions of types which in other circumstances might be seriously wrong. The question would remain as to whether a line may be drawn between things done intentionally and things done knowingly.

It is part of the business of theory of action to provide a framework of concepts which are themselves as neutral as possible but in terms of which moral issues may be discussed with something approaching precision. For this reason, at least, it seems desirable to accept Sam's point of view and reserve the term "intentionally" for cases where the agent aimed at doing what he is said to have done intentionally.[8]

"AIMING AT"   Another way of saying the agent aimed at doing an A is to say that an A, or doing an A, was his purpose in acting. Saying this is sometimes confused with saying the agent had a reason—understood in terms of antecedents—for doing an A. But what *is* the difference? And is it not the case that having an A as one's purpose in acting involves something which precedes the action?

The difference is clearest in cases where the act-type A is in the agent's repertoire. Sal's kicking the door in anger will serve as an example, for if "kicking the door" is not in her repertoire, "kicking a specified nearby object" surely is, and the specified nearby object may be the door. We said before that she need have had no reason whatever for kicking it, yet kicking it is what she "aimed at." We can regard this as a matter of definition, following from the fact that her volition was itself an event aimed at causing her foot to make forcible contact with the door. That is, her volition had "kicking the specified nearby object" as its object, and volitions with this object "normally" cause her foot to connect forcibly with whatever the specified nearby object happens to be.

Sam's extending his arm out the window was generated, we supposed, by a volition with "extending one's arm" as its object. Volitions with this object "normally" cause extension of his arm, so we can say his volition was aimed at achieving this result, and so Sam himself was aiming at extending his arm. Again, given only this information, we are not forced to

---

8 In legal contexts, acting knowingly is generally considered enough for "intention." Meiland, *Nature of Intention*, pp. 7–12, speaks of "nonpurposive" intentions. Alvin I. Goldman, *A Theory of Human Action* (Englewood Cliffs, N.J.: Prentice-Hall, Inc., 1970; Princeton Paperback, 1976) [hereafter referred to as *THA*], pp. 57, 59–60, speaks of "nonintentional" actions as including those foreseen but not expected to be a means to the agent's end. See also Anscombe, *Intention*, p. 42, and the references cited in the preceding footnote.

suppose he extended his arm because of any reason he may have had for extending his arm.

If we inquire why it is that volitions to extend the arm normally result in the arm's getting extended, we may encounter various feedback mechanisms between the arm and a monitoring process initiated by the volition. These mechanisms account for the fact that movement stops when the arm is extended, and various "corrective" measures would have been taken in the face of certain kinds of obstacles. The role of these mechanisms adds to the sense in which the volition was aimed at getting the arm extended; but their operation is still nothing *preceding* the action itself.

Turning to act-types not in the agent's repertoire, we find that saying the agent "aimed at doing an A" does commit us to something prior to the action. But this is so even where the agent merely "did an A knowingly." Sam, for example, watered the flowers; and we have assumed the objects of his volitions were "extending one's arm" and "turning one's wrist so as to invert the object in one's hand." We may suppose, then, that the act-type "watering the flowers" itself was not in his repertoire. Now he watered the flowers knowingly. This implies knowledge in advance that his extending his arm and turning his wrist would generate his watering the flowers. What Sam did intentionally, what he was aiming at, was simply emptying the can; and here also, we must say he knew in advance that his extending his arm and turning his wrist would generate his emptying the can.

The difference here between "knowingly" and "aiming at" is not the existence of the knowledge in advance, but the role played by it. Sam did what he did, the volitions to extend his arm and turn his wrist occurred, *because* of his knowledge that he would thereby empty the can. He did not act, the volitions did not occur, "because" he knew that he would thereby water the flowers.

This account of the difference between "aiming at doing an A" and "(merely) doing an A knowingly," where A is not in the agent's repertoire, implies that the agent does after all "act for a reason." But we are not back to the suggestion that intentionally doing an A involves having a reason *for doing an A*. Sam's awareness that he would be emptying the can if he extended his arm and turned his wrist is at most his reason for extending his arm and turning his wrist. It is not his reason, nor could it be anyone's reason, for emptying the can. In general, where A is not in the agent's repertoire, the agent "aimed at doing an A" if for some B in his repertoire he willed to do a B (in part) because he believed (knew, was aware) that he would thereby do an A. This belief we can say was the agent's reason (or part of it) *for doing a B,* but not for doing an A.

There is no implication that an agent who aimed at doing an A had any reason for doing so.

Failure to appreciate the fact that an agent's reason for doing a B need not be his reason for doing an A, even when his doing a B and his doing an A are the same action, underlies much of the confusion between an agent's "reason" and his "purpose." To forestall this confusion as much as possible, we are understanding "reasons" in the manner illustrated earlier, in terms of beliefs and desires prior to the action; and instead of using the word "purpose," we will here speak exclusively of what the agent "aimed at."

Our account of "aiming at" in terms of the role played by certain of the agent's beliefs can replace our earlier talk of "means" and "ends." The doctor of our second example removed the uterus by performing a sequence of actions of a number of types in his repertoire ("making an incision," etc.). The sequence of volitions occurred *because* he believed his performing this sequence of actions would generate his removing the uterus. The belief was (part of) his reason for performing these actions, not for removing the uterus; but the role played by this belief shows that he aimed at removing the uterus. He also believed that he would cause the fetus to die if he did these things; but the volitions did not occur because of *this* belief. In no way did he aim at killing the fetus.

What shows that the doctor also aimed at saving the woman? Perhaps we can say the sequence of volitions occurred because he believed he would save the woman by doing these things. But perhaps his thinking would be more accurately reflected if we say he aimed at removing the uterus because he believed he would save the woman thereby. We should allow ourselves to say in general, then, that an agent "aimed at doing an A" if for some B, he aimed at doing a B because he believed his doing a B would generate his doing an A.

There is another kind of case which must be considered. Imagine an agent in New York who intentionally drops a letter bearing a Los Angeles address into a mailbox. Assume he does it because he believes he will thereby get it delivered to the address in Los Angeles; this shows that he aims at getting it delivered there. Suppose that all letters from New York to California make a stop in Chicago, but that the agent does not know this. He has no belief that by dropping the letter in the box he will get it to Chicago, so he does not drop the letter in the box "because" of this belief. It follows that he does not aim at getting the letter to Chicago—and since aiming at is necessary for acting intentionally, it follows that he does not intentionally send the letter to Chicago. This seems correct. But now suppose that just before he drops the letter in the box, he learns that all such letters are brought first to Chicago. As he lets go of the letter, he knows nonobservationally that he is sending it on its way to Chicago. Shall we also say that he is aiming at this, and that he is doing it intentionally?

The doctor could claim that causing the fetus to die was no part of his intention; to the contrary, he would wish it could be saved. But the death of the fetus was not a means to the woman's recovery. Here, it seems the agent can no longer claim that it is no part of his intention to have the letter brought to Chicago. The route to Los Angeles, he has learned, does pass through Chicago. Insofar as he aims at getting the letter to Los Angeles, he must also aim at getting it to Chicago. But his (newly acquired) belief that by dropping the letter in the box he will get it brought to Chicago plays no role in his action. He does not drop the letter in the box *because* of this belief; he was ready to drop the letter in the box before he had the belief. We must formulate our definition of "aiming at" to accommodate cases of this kind.

A complete account, then, will have three parts and look like this:

(1) An agent x aimed at doing an A if and only if:
   (i) x willed to do an A; or
   (ii) for some B, x aimed at doing a B because he believed his doing a B would generate his doing an A; or
   (iii) for some B and some C, x aimed at doing a B because he believed his doing a B would generate his doing a C; and x believed at the time that if his doing a B indeed generated his doing a C, his doing a C would have been generated by his doing an A. (But x did not aim at doing a B because of this latter belief.)

Clause (iii) covers cases like the one just described. The agent aimed at dropping the letter in the box (= B) because he believed his doing so would generate his getting the letter to Los Angeles (= C). The agent also believed at the time that if he indeed got the letter to Los Angeles by dropping it into the box, his doing the former would have been generated by his getting the letter to Chicago (= A). The agent did not, however, aim at dropping the letter in the box because of this latter belief.

"BECAUSE HE BELIEVED . . ." The word "because" that we have been using and that appears in clauses (ii) and (iii) of (1) needs explanation. Not just any connection between the relevant beliefs and volitions will do. Imagine a powerful mind reader who dislikes agents' acting without knowledge of the consequences of their actions. Seeing the doctor about to remove the woman's uterus, the mind reader checks to see if the doctor is aware that he will thereby cause the fetus to die. The doctor is aware, so the mind reader does not interfere. Had the doctor lacked the belief (awareness) that the fetus would die, the mind reader (who is *very* powerful) would have prevented the volitions from occurring. There is a sense, then, in which the volitions occurred "because" the doctor had this belief. But we do not want this to imply that the doctor aimed at causing the fetus to die.

In Chapter 1 a similar bit of science fiction pointed up a similar kind of problem. Given a case of an event occurring "because" of a desire, for the case to be one of action it is necessary that the desire and the event be connected "in a certain characteristic way," to use Alvin Goldman's phrase. We eventually explained that way as involving the occurrence of a volition, linking the desire to the event. Now, there are events, states, and processes which may link belief to volition: decisions, states of intending, processes of deliberation, and so on. But we cannot solve our present problem by explaining the "because" of (1) in terms of the occurrence of these phenomena. They do *not* always occur. We have already argued that not every intentional action is preceded by a state of intending. Even where there is prior intent, there may never have been a decision or other definite formation of the intention. A person may intend all day to eat supper in the evening, without ever having *decided* to do so. Finally, it seems that decisions and choices may be made without anything worthy of the name "deliberation" preceding them.

A *verbal* solution suggests itself: the way in which belief must be linked to volition for the "because" of (1) to apply is that way, whatever it is, which allows us to say the belief is the agent's *reason* for the ensuing action. Recall, for example, that Sam's belief that his extending his arm and turning his wrist will generate his emptying the can is (part of) his reason for extending his arm and turning his wrist. This is of some value, if only for indicating the difficulty remaining. We do not have a convincing and thorough account of the nature of reasons for acting, or the way in which they are connected to the actions for which they are reasons. The next chapter focuses on just one of the controversial issues, whether the connection is causal or not. Important as this issue is for understanding how human actions are explained, it only minimally enhances our understanding of what reasons are. Suppose, for example, that Sam extended his arm and turned his wrist "because" he believed that George Washington was the first president of the United States. Does this make any sense? *Could* this belief have been Sam's reason for acting, or even part of his reason? What seems needed is a full theory of practical reasoning—for example, deliberating about what to do. This would include not only an account of what deliberative processes and related phenomena are actually like, but an account of when the reasoning that takes place may be considered *good* reasoning. All these inquiries are beyond the scope of this book.[9]

Volitions were introduced as functionally characterized events. Perhaps the way in which belief and volition must be connected for the former to be the agent's reason for the latter can also be functionally characterized. This characterization would be based on a description of how the various phenomena mentioned in the preceding two paragraphs are related to one another and to other associated phenomena, especially when the agent's practical reasoning is "good" from some standpoint.

One "associated phenomenon" worth comment is the agent's awareness of his reason for acting. Sam knows whether he is watering the flowers or just emptying the can—that is, he knows whether or not he is aiming at the former as well as the latter. By (1), this means he knows whether or not he has extended his arm and turned his wrist "because" of his awareness that he would thereby water the flowers. How does he know this? Our explanation of Sam's nonobservational knowledge that he is watering the flowers, even if unintentionally, appealed to the direct contribution made by a volition to do an A to the agent's awareness that he is doing an A. It seems that when a belief is connected to a volition in the way of which we have been speaking, this very situation leads "directly" to awareness by the agent that he is acting because of that belief. This fact (or a more accurate formulation of it) should be as important in an explanation of the "because" of (1) as was the connection between volition and awareness of acting in the explanation of what volitions are.

IS KNOWLEDGE NECESSARY TO ACTING INTENTIONALLY?

Of the three factors that have been proposed as important in an explanation of "doing an A intentionally," we have eliminated from consideration the agent's having a reason to do an A, and we have decided that it is not enough that the agent does an A knowingly, that he has nonobservational knowledge that he is doing an A. It is essential that he be "aiming at" doing an A, as this phrase is defined by (1). We must now consider whether it is necessary at all that the agent have this nonobservational knowledge. Perhaps "doing an A intentionally" can be completely identified with "doing an A, where this is what one is aiming at."

Perhaps there is no compelling argument either way, and there are two slightly different things that might be meant by saying an agent did an A intentionally. It might be meant just that this is what he was aiming at, and it might be implied also that he knew nonobservationally that

9 See Bibliography for some relevant literature.

he was doing it. A third slightly stricter conception would require also that the agent knew he was aiming at it. Finally, in the same tolerant spirit we might reinstate as a fourth view that it is "aiming at" which is inessential, and "doing an A intentionally" can be identified with "doing an A knowingly."

A qualification is necessary, however, in any conception which does require some knowledge. The requirement cannot really be for knowledge "that he is doing an A," because of cases where the agent cannot be sure while acting that he is *succeeding* in doing what he is aiming at. As a simple example, consider an agent typing a letter with ten carbons. He may not know that all ten are getting made. But if they do get made, then he has made even the tenth "intentionally." Now he did believe and know that all ten *might* be getting made, and the example shows that this is enough. In general, to do an A intentionally it is often enough that one has nonobservational knowledge that one *might* be doing an A. (Notice that (1), our analysis of "aiming at," must be weakened in a similar way. For as (1) stands, an agent "aimed at" typing ten carbons only if he believed his action *would* generate his typing ten carbons. He may not have been so confident.)

Another case illustrates a second difficulty for a conception of "doing an A intentionally" which requires the agent to know he is doing an A. Sam is aiming at watering the flowers, believes nonobservationally, confidently, and correctly that he is doing so, but is in error about *how* he is doing so. The water from the can is prevented by a clear plastic sheet from reaching the flowers, but his extended arm causes a photocell-operated mechanism to activate a sprinkler system. Many philosophers would say Sam does not really *know* he is watering the flowers, precisely because he is not watering them in the way he thinks he is. Shall we conclude that he is not watering them intentionally?[10]

Note finally that any conception of acting intentionally which does require some knowledge may prove incompatible with one of the claims mentioned at the beginning of this chapter, that all action is intentional. For whenever there is a volition, there is an action; but if knowledge is required for acting intentionally, there might be an action which is of *no* type A such that the agent is doing an A intentionally. The agent may have no knowledge whatsoever of the volition or of anything generated by it. But if acting intentionally is identified with aiming at, the claim would seem to be true. For there is no action without a volition, and no volition without an object. If the volition is a volition to do an A, then

10 Cf. Roderick M. Chisholm, "Freedom and Action," in Keith Lehrer, ed., *Freedom and Determinism* (New York: Random House, Inc., 1966), pp. 28–44; excerpted in Myles Brand, ed., *The Nature of Human Action* (Glenview, Ill.: Scott, Foresman and Company, 1970), pp. 283–92.

by (1), the agent is aiming at doing an A, even if he has no reason for doing so and no awareness that he is. (An apparent casualty of identifying acting intentionally with aiming at is our formula that intention is a matter of "how the agent thought of the action." Perhaps the agent did not think in any way at all about what he did, though he was aiming at something! On the other hand, perhaps aiming at something can itself be regarded as a kind of thinking about the action which actually gets performed, even if it is not of the type aimed at.)

It may be doubted that there could really be an action of which the agent had no knowledge whatsoever. In particular, it may seem that the agent will inevitably know what he is aiming at. Suppose the agent is aiming at doing an A, where A is *not* in his repertoire. Then for some B in his repertoire, he is aiming at B because he believes that his doing a B will (or might) generate his doing an A. Is it possible that he does not also believe that he is in fact acting on this belief, doing a B in the hope or expectation that he will thereby do an A? Have we not said above, in discussing the "because" here, that this situation just does lead directly to this awareness by the agent?

In the other direction, it seems no mistake is possible. That is, if the agent does believe that he is doing a B because he hopes or expects his doing so to generate his doing an A, then this belief *cannot* be in error. (Well, perhaps he is only trying unsuccessfully to do a B; but it will be said, he is still doing this for the reason he thinks he is.) Suppose Sam tells us sincerely that he is watering the flowers intentionally, and not merely emptying the can with the unintended-though-foreseen consequence that the flowers get watered. Can we or anyone tell Sam he is wrong, that this is not in fact what he is aiming at? Many philosophers think Sam cannot be mistaken, and have regarded this element of infallibility as a centrally important feature of an agent's knowledge of what he is doing intentionally.

But if an agent's belief that he is aiming at doing an A really is infallible, with no possibility of mistake, why suppose his belief that he is *not* aiming at doing an A might be mistaken? If we must believe Sam when he tells us sincerely that he *is* intentionally watering the flowers, how can we doubt him when he tells us equally sincerely that he is aiming only at emptying the can and does not care about the flowers? We shall not try to answer this question, or pass final judgment on the first alleged infallibility. We merely note that many philosophers who would accept Sam's infallibility in the first case are still willing to recognize the possibility of an unconscious reason, hence intention, in the second case. Others may be persuaded that error is possible even in the first case, however rare and difficult to imagine.

If A is in the agent's repertoire, can the agent fail to know that he is aiming at doing an A? By (1), he aims at doing an A if a volition to do an A occurs. By the functional characterization of volitions, a volition to do an A "normally" causes the agent to believe he is doing an A. But we have not described any *abnormal* cases in which the belief would clearly be absent. If, for example, the agent willed to do an A from force of habit while his attention was elsewhere, there may be grounds for saying the agent "believes" he is doing an A even though he is not *consciously thinking* anything we would represent as "I am doing an A." This again is an issue on which we shall not try to pass judgment. Accordingly, we cannot label as strictly "true" or "false" the claim that all action is intentional. But our rehearsal of the possibilities should make it clear why the claim is at worst *nearly* true, on any of the conceptions of acting intentionally that are discussed in this section.

THEORIES OF INTENDING   If a person does intend to do an A at a more-or-less definite future time or expected future occasion, he is in a state which will *lead him to do it* when he believes the time or the occasion has arrived (and when it does, the agent will do an A intentionally). Some attempts to describe more precisely this link between intending and eventual action have made a fairly commonplace phenomenon seem mysterious: a person intends to do an A yet fails to do it when the time comes, though he has not changed his mind and nothing prevents him.[11] This may be called *irresolute behavior*. A satisfactory theory of intending should recognize and allow for its possibility.

If a person intends to do an A, he generally believes that he will do an A, and some philosophers have thought that a careful account of this belief and its content is all that is needed to understand what intending is. This approach may help demystify irresolute behavior, since it allows for a weaker connection between intending and eventual action, but it raises puzzles and difficulties of its own. When shall we say that an agent's claim that he will do an A expresses his intention already formed, and when does it express a mere prediction of his future behavior? Or is there no difference? If there is no difference (and perhaps even if there is), it would be impossible for a person to know in advance of deciding (forming the intention) to do something that he was *going* to decide to

[11] This person's failure to act is akin to the more frequently discussed failure of a person to do something he not merely intends, but believes it would be *best* to do, or believes it is *obligatory* to do. In these last two cases, the person suffers from "weakness of the will," or *akrasia*, as it is called after the Greek of Socrates, Plato, and Aristotle. See Bibliography for references. In Chapter 6 we will discuss autonomy, a psychological feature quite opposite to both irresoluteness and akrasia.

do it, and eventually do it. This implication may at first seem true and harmless enough. But in a paper which sparked a good deal of controversy, Carl Ginet turned it into an argument against determinism (hence in favor of some free will doctrines): if Sam's future decisions and actions are already determined, it ought to be possible for someone to predict them confidently. But then Sam himself could be given the information, in which case he would know what he was going to do before reaching the decision to do it. This (allegedly) is impossible, so his future actions, at least those which will stem from decisions of his, must not be determined.[12]

In the next section we will discuss the belief or knowledge about what one is going to do that is associated with intending, to see if this argument can even get started. Following that we will return to the question of the link between intending and eventual action and come to a rough understanding of what it is to intend to do something—an understanding which will clearly leave room for irresoluteness and other reasons for nonexecution of intentions. In the balance of this section we will dispose of the view that intending is just a kind of wanting.

Often enough a person who intends to do an A will say "I want to do an A" as readily as "I intend to do an A." And if intending *were* just a kind of wanting, the questions and puzzles we have mentioned would be no harder to solve than questions we face anyway, about the link between desire and eventual action, and a person's beliefs or knowledge about what he "wants" to do. But there are differences, even on the surface, which show that this simple theory of intending cannot be correct.

Wanting admits of degrees, and a person can simultaneously and consciously want two things he knows are incompatible; intending has neither of these characteristics. Sam can want to eat some chocolates he is offered *and* want to keep trim, and one of these desires may be stronger than the other. But if he *intends* to eat some of the chocolates, knowing this will cause him to become overweight, it hardly seems possible to say he also intends to keep trim. Even if we allow him both intentions, it does not seem right to say that one is stronger than the other. More likely, we would say that when he formed the intention to eat the chocolates he temporarily forgot or even abandoned his intention to keep trim. This is evidence not that the latter was weak, or weaker than the former but that it was not a very *firm* intention. Nor need the intention to eat the chocolates have been any firmer. If he were distracted for a moment —say, by a telephone call—he might simply forget to eat the chocolates afterward as readily as he had previously forgotten or abandoned his intention to stay away from them.

---

[12] Carl Ginet, "Can the Will Be Caused?" *Philosophical Review*, LXXI (1962), 49–55.

These differences and some others between wanting and intending may not hold for special kinds of wanting. If we say, for example, that Sam "wanted on balance" to keep trim, or "wanted, all things considered," to eat the chocolates, it may be that we cannot say he also wanted "on balance" or "all things considered" something he knew was incompatible, even to a lesser degree. But if "wanting on balance" and "wanting, all things considered" are really kinds of wanting, it seems they must have some of the characteristic ties of wanting to feeling and emotion. A person generally feels satisfaction at doing what he wants, frustration at being prevented. While the action still lies in the future, he is likely to feel joy upon learning that he will soon have an opportunity to do it, and he is likely to feel disappointment upon learning the opposite. None of this need be true of intending: it is possible to intend to do A without caring at all whether, or when, one will succeed. An agent completely devoid of emotions, who never cares about what he does or experiences, is a grotesque caricature of a normal human being; yet it seems possible to imagine such beings, and to imagine them forming and executing intentions. Alienated soldiers following their orders and disinterested administrators and bureaucrats may be approximations to such agents. On a grander scale, some would say that God, while devoid of emotions in any human sense, can still be properly spoken of as having intentions and carrying them out. If so, intending is not a kind of wanting.

KNOWLEDGE OF ONE'S FUTURE ACTIONS

A person who intends to do an A will often *know* and not merely *believe* that he will do an A. In overstated form, then, there are three theses to be considered:

(1) If a person x intends to do an A, then x knows that he will do an A.

(2) If x knows that he will do an A, then x intends to do an A.

(3) Knowing that one will do an A and intending to do an A are the same thing.

Notice that (1) and (2) do not entail (3): equilateral triangles are equiangular, and equiangular triangles are equilateral, but being equilateral and being equiangular are not the same thing. We will see that more cautious and precise versions of (1) and (2) are apparently true, but that a parallel restatement of (3) is still false.

Against (1), it is sufficient to note that we often fail to do things we intend to do. Even apart from irresoluteness, we change our minds, forget, and find ourselves unable. At an extreme, an agent may simply die before having a chance to do what he had every intention of doing and would have done, had he lived. But if he never does it, then it is incorrect to say he ever knew he would do it, so (1) is false. Perhaps we would get a true statement from (1) if we substituted "believes" for "knows." Some think an agent could "intend to do A" even if he believed on the basis of powerful evidence that he will never succeed; to accommodate this possibility we should add the words "or at least try" to the revised (1). But there is *some* dimension of certainty about one's future action implied by intending, which this revision of (1) fails to capture, even if it is true. (It may not be. Perhaps an agent who believes he will never succeed should be described not as "intending to do an A," but merely as "hoping," or as "intending to *try* to do an A." But we shall make the suggested revision of (1).)

The important point seems to be this. A person would not come to have an intention in the first place if he did not expect things to develop in such a way that execution of the intention (or the attempt) will be both possible and in accord with what he will then be minded to do (or try). If Sam intends to go for a walk in an hour, he is in a position to claim, "If things are as I think, and continue to be as I anticipate, I will go for a walk in an hour." If he changes his mind, or someone locks the doors, then he or the world will not have turned out as he anticipated, so his claim is not falsified.[13] If he knows he is lazy, or has other reason to suspect that he would irresolutely simply fail to go for the walk, then his intention to go for a walk may include subsidiary intentions to rouse himself in the interim and exert special "willpower" when the hour is up. If he is uncertain that these measures will suffice, he is nonetheless in a position to claim, "If things turn out as I now anticipate, I will go for a walk in an hour or *at least have tried*." ("Trying" here covers the measures taken in advance and at the time to *get* himself to start walking, so the claim is not falsified even if no actual volitions to walk occur at the time.)

Sam does expect things to turn out as he anticipates, so (forgetting for the moment about "trying") he does believe that he will go for a walk in an hour. But he has something stronger than mere belief. If things are now as he thinks and continue to be so, and he does go for a walk in an hour, then we can say in retrospect that he *knew* he was going to go for a walk in an hour. Even if things turn out otherwise, his belief is of a kind that *would* have been knowledge if only they had not turned out otherwise. Sam is sensitive to this status of his belief; in expressing it, he would not say "I believe I will go for a walk," but just "I will go for a walk." He may not *have* knowledge, but he is in effect *claiming* knowledge of his future action.

---

[13] If he thinks someone may lock the doors, then his intention is not to "go for a walk," but the *conditional intention* to "go for a walk if no one locks the doors." If he thinks there is a good chance he will change his mind, his intention is to "go for a walk if I do not change my mind." Conditional intentions are discussed by Meiland, *Nature of Intention*, pp. 15–34.

A more interesting revision of (1), then, is the following:

(1′) If x intends to do an A, then x believes and would claim to know that he will intentionally do an A, or at least try.

We should bear in mind the possibility that there are intentions which are wholly unconscious. But then, there may also be beliefs which are wholly unconscious, so (1′) may not be in jeopardy on this account. And so long as we do not press the word "would" too far ("*When* would he claim . . . ?" "What if he lacked the necessary vocabulary, or even the concepts?"), (1′) seems to be true.

What about the converse of (1′), or (2) as it stands? Their truth would support those who see no difference between statements expressing intentions and statements expressing predictions of one's future behavior, and would open the door to arguments like Ginet's against determinism.

But the knowledge or belief of a person who intends to do an A differs significantly from that of a person who merely predicts that he will do an A. A prediction is based on evidence which amount to reasons for expecting the action to take place; and the evidence comes from observation. Sue may predict that Sam will go for a walk in an hour. This involves more, of course, than a prediction that he will have the ability to go for a walk in an hour; she must have reasons for expecting the appropriate volitions to occur. A reason might be: "He has gone for a walk every Thursday at 2:30 for the last six months, and it is now 1:30 on Thursday." Or more complicated: "He has been working hard for three hours straight and has never been known to go longer than four hours without a break, and given the beautiful weather, taking a walk is the likeliest form his 'break' will take." Sam himself does not make comparable use of reasons for expecting himself to go for a walk in an hour. He may merely look at his watch and say: "Another hour and it will be time for my walk," or "Another hour and I will have had it; it's beautiful out—why don't I take a walk? Yes; that's what I'll do!" In the second case, he *decides* to go for a walk; the knowledge of what he will do comes at the same time the intention is formed. In the first case, he already has the intention to go for a walk at 2:30 as he does every Thursday, and glancing at his watch merely tells him when 2:30 is, in relation to the present moment. Again, the specific intention to go for a walk "in an hour" and the knowledge that he will do this come at the same time. In neither case does he infer on the basis of his past and current behavior and circumstances—or even on the basis of "internal observation" of his thoughts and feelings—that he will take a walk in an hour. If anything, facts about his behavior, etc., serve him as reasons for acting—or forming the intention to act—in a certain way, not as reasons for expecting that he will act in a certain way, as they serve Sue. His knowledge of how he will act, of what he has formed the intention to do, is not based directly on these or any other external facts at all. Like knowledge of what one is intentionally doing, it is nonobservational.

This shows that we may insert the word "nonobservationally" before "believes" in (1′). And if we ignore some unusual kinds of nonobservational knowledge (e.g., a brain surgeon simply implanting the knowledge in Sam), the following seems a correct replacement for (2):

(2′) If x nonobservationally believes and would claim to know that he will intentionally do an A, or at least try, then he intends to do an A (or at least to try).

A "nonobservational belief" is one not wholly based on observation as predictions are. Sam's belief may be partly based on observation, if, for example, his belief that he will be *able* to go for a walk in an hour's time is based on observation.

We can now see that there is no genuine impossibility in knowing that one is going to do something and only afterwards forming the intention to do it. Imagine that Sue confronts Sam in the morning with the prediction that he will go for a walk at 2:30. (She bases this on his known work plans, information how the day's weather will be, and so on.) Sam knows that Sue's predictions have always been correct, so he comes to believe that he will do this. The belief is based wholly on observation—Sue's testimony, and his past evidence of her accuracy—so he does not yet intend to go for a walk at 2:30. Now at 1:30, he looks at his watch, and remembers that in an hour he is destined to go for a walk. He may at this moment form the *intention* to do so. "I'm going to go for a walk in an hour. Come to think of it, I've been working for a long time, and another hour is about all I can stand. It's beautiful out; taking a walk is an excellent idea. That's what I'll do!" From this point on, his knowledge that he will go for a walk at 2:30 is not *wholly* based on observation as predictions are. He has formed the intention to do this, and so one of the sources of his knowledge is nonobservational.[14]

INTENDING AND DOING

A revision of (3) analogous to (1′) and (2′) would be this:

(3′) Intending to do an A is just nonobservationally believing (and being ready to claim knowledge) that one will do an A, or at least try.

This view suffers from at least two serious defects. It leaves us with no

---

[14] Goldman, *THA*, pp. 170–96, offers a thorough and illuminating discussion of this and related issues. Goldman claims that it *is* impossible to *deliberate* about what to do if one already knows what one is going to do (p. 194). Sam's soliloquy here may be a counterexample. Even if not, it seems the impossibility is at most *psychological* rather than conceptual or logical. See also Richard Taylor, *Action and Purpose* (Englewood Cliffs, N.J.: Prentice-Hall, Inc., 1966), pp. 174–76.

obvious direction in which to look for the nonobservational source of the agent's belief; and it suggests no plausible account of how or why intending naturally leads to action.

Sometimes belief that one will do an A does lead to one's doing an A. William James described a person who (successfully) leaps a precipice only because he first gets himself to believe he can and will.[15] In the story of Sam and Sue just told, perhaps Sam's belief that he would go for a walk also played a role in leading him to do it. But in the first case, the intention is already formed and leads to the agent's efforts to get himself to believe he will succeed. In the second case, the belief leads to the thinking which results in the intention. Neither case supports (3′).

We must say that the nonobservational belief of which (1′) and (2′) speak *accompanies* and is not the same state as intending to do an A. Moreover, the belief is caused or explained by the actual state of intending, much as an agent's belief that he is doing an A is caused by his willing to do an A (or, where A is not in his repertoire, by his aiming at doing an A). This is the "nonobservational source" of the belief.

What, then, is this "actual state of intending to do an A"? Some would again wish to invoke a kind of wanting; in their view, "intending to do an A" is a combination of wanting to do an A with believing (presumably as a result of this wanting) that one will do an A, or try. But our previous objections to identifying intending with a kind of wanting are not removed by combining the latter with an appropriate belief.

Intending to do an A is a mental state not identifiable with any other or set of others for which we have a familiar name. Following our approach with volitions and "aiming at," we might try to characterize it functionally, describing its relations with other mental states and events. "Intending to do an A" could then be defined as the state standing in these relations to these others. We will offer only some highlights of such a characterization.

To some extent, intending to do an A on an expected future occasion O is parallel to a volition to do an A. It is a state "likely" to obtain when (and only when) the agent "wants or has other reason" to do an A on O. We may say it "directly causes, or contributes to causing" the agent's nonobservational belief that he will do an A on O.[16] And it "normally" leads to the agent's intentionally doing an A on O.[17]

15 William James, *Essays in Pragmatism,* ed. Alburey Castell (New York: Hafner Publishing Company, 1966), p. 27.

16 More accurately, since we regard causation as a relation exclusively between events, the onset of the state—formation of the intention—causes the onset of the belief, and cessation of the state may cause cessation of the belief. See footnote 10 of Chapter 1.

17 This parallel accounts for the attractiveness of Wilfrid Sellars's view (see Bibliography to Chapter 1) that a volition to do an A just is an intention to do an A "now." Sellars's view blurs the distinction between states and events, and between intending and acting intentionally. But see the concluding section of this chapter, on intentional omissions.

A fuller account of when the state is likely to obtain would have to consider the relations between intending, deciding, choosing, and deliberating. It must also be said that the state will "normally" obtain only if (and only so long as) the agent has an appropriate conception of the interim between the present moment and the expected future occasion O. Earlier we expressed this by saying the agent "expects things to develop in such a way that execution of the intention (or the attempt) will be both possible and in accord with what he will be minded to do" when O arrives. He need not believe that he will encounter no obstacle, or pressure to change his mind. But if he does expect obstacles, his conception of the interim is "appropriate" only if he also believes that he has the ability to do, by the time O arrives, anything and everything necessary so that when O does arrive he will have the ability to do an A. (See preceding chapter for discussion of ability to do something by some later time.) And if he does expect pressure to change his mind, he must not expect that he will actually be convinced.[18]

It is of interest that this conception of the interim may have large gaps and be very indefinite. The occasion O may be conceived of as vaguely as "whenever I happen to think the time has come," though it is necessary that the agent believe he will think "the time has come" some time in the future. (Otherwise, instead of intending to "do an A on O," he has the conditional intention to "do an A if he should happen to think an appropriate time has come.") The agent may envision several ways in which it might happen that he has the ability to do an A on O, and be uncertain which way will be actual. For example, Sam intends to see a movie in Boston tomorrow night, but does not yet know how he is getting to Boston. He believes, however, that there is at least one way open to him and that he will be able to identify the available ways and choose one in enough time to get there before the movie starts. He may be wrong, but until he finds this out, his conception of the interim is "appropriate" and enables him to have this intention.

It can even be that an agent intends to do an A at a time when he does not know how to do an A and may not fully understand what A is. Jack Meiland discusses an agent John who:

. . . overhears one man say to another: "I'd pay a very large sum of money to anyone who would build me a Sheraton sideboard." John knows neither what a sideboard is nor what the term "Sheraton" means. He does not even know that

---

[18] In the special case where the agent has *committed* himself formally or informally to doing an A on O, he may have formed what James W. Hall, *Self-Prediction and Free Will* (unpublished doctoral dissertation, Johns Hopkins University, 1975), calls an "intention to maintain the intention" of doing an A on O. This means, roughly, that he has taken or intends to take steps to prevent himself from being influenced by certain kinds of pressures and reasons for abandoning the intention to do an A on O.

a piece of furniture is being talked about, nor does he know that Sheraton sideboards are made out of wood. Perhaps he also does not know what the word "build" means. But John needs the sum of money mentioned.[19]

Meiland argues that John does know that what he has to do to earn the money is an action of a type called "building a Sheraton sideboard," and that this is enough of an understanding of this act-type to enable John to intend to build a Sheraton sideboard. In our terms, the point is that John's conception of the interim provides or allows for his finding out what is involved in this act-type called "building a Sheraton sideboard" and in acquiring whatever skills, materials, and so on that will prove necessary. John may be hopelessly naive in having this conception. Perhaps as soon as he learns that Sheraton sideboards are made of wood, he will give up, because he already knows he is a terrible carpenter. But he does not know this yet, and perhaps foolishly, does not admit the possibility into his conception of the interim. He is still capable, then, of intending to build a Sheraton sideboard.[20]

Now we can describe more fully the way in which "intending to do an A on O" is a state which "normally" leads to the agent's intentionally doing an A on O. So long as he is in this state, and so long as events transpire in a way not ruled out by his conception of the interim, at each juncture when, according to his belief at the time, his doing an A on O requires an action of a certain type, he will intentionally perform an action of that type (or try to perform one), culminating in his intentionally doing an A when O arrives.

If it turns out that the agent is unable to successfully perform some action he believes required, events have ceased to transpire in accord with his conception. Assuming he realizes this, he can "normally" be expected to cease being in the state of "intending to do an A on O." Similarly, if he finds himself with an overriding reason for not doing an A on O, or for not taking one of the preliminary steps he believes required—he did not expect this to happen. There may be other reasons for cessation of the state of intending. In particular, all may go well right up to the occasion O, and the state just cease to obtain, for none of the reasons already suggested. It would be true that the agent had intended to do an A on O, that he had not changed his mind, and in no way lacked the ability to do an A when O arrived. This would be a case of irresolute-

---

19 Meiland, *Nature of Intention*, p. 47.

20 In the same way, an agent can intend to do something impossible, like drawing a round square, until he realizes the impossibility. And if he believes it impossible, he cannot intend to do it, even if his belief is mistaken. Note that in the latter case, the agent may be able to *try* to do it. Suppose Sam believes his watch is unbreakable. To convince a doubter, he may "try to break it" by hitting it with a hammer. Cf. Thalberg, *Enigmas of Agency*, p. 103.

ness; and while it would still have to be explained, we have at least seen that the concept of intending is compatible with such cases.

INTENTIONAL OMISSIONS   Our discussion of intention has been based on distinguishing sharply between intending and doing something intentionally. We will close this chapter with a look at a case which blurs the distinction somewhat: intending not to do an A on O, and intentionally not doing an A.

Roderick Chisholm offers the following example. One man greets another and the second man does not respond. His failure may have been intentional; perhaps he had the further intention of snubbing the first man, of insulting him by failing to respond to his greeting.[21]

The man may have intended this in advance. He believed they would meet and the other man would greet him, and he intended to fail to respond on this occasion. All that we have said about "intending to do an A on O" applies, except that we do not understand the end of the matter, his "intentionally doing an A when O arrives." For the point is that on this occasion *no* volition occurs; or at least it is not necessary that any occur in order for it to be true that he does not respond to the greeting. It is necessary only that no volition occurs which generates his responding to the greeting.

Chisholm's own suggestion is approximately that the man considers responding, but does not. The nonoccurrence of a volition relevant to responding is intentional, then, because if the agent had done what he considered doing, a relevant volition would have occurred. A minor defect with this reasoning is that Chisholm apparently thinks the "considering" must take place at the time of the omission. The agent may have done all his considering earlier, when he first formed the intention to snub the other.

A more serious defect is that no *link* is postulated between the considering and the nonoccurrence of any relevant volition. The letter of Chisholm's suggestion leaves open the possibility that the agent considered responding, in fact decided that he *would* respond, but simply failed to do so, perhaps because of some brain malfunction.

A more promising suggestion is that whether he "considered" anything or not, the agent was on this occasion in what we may call a state of intending (now) not to respond, and his being in this state explains why no relevant volition occurred.[22]

---

[21] Roderick M. Chisholm, "The Agent as Cause," in Myles Brand and Douglas Walton, eds., *Action Theory* (Dordrecht: D. Reidel Publishing Company, 1976), p. 207.

[22] We do not say the state *caused* the nonoccurrence, because we regard causation as a relation exclusively between events. The state is not an event and so cannot be a cause (cf. footnote 16). And the nonoccurrence is not an event—it is the failure of an

As for the sort of "explanation" afforded, suppose first that the man felt some impulse to respond. After all, one greeting elicits another almost automatically from all but the most asocial of us. But if, as in the case under discussion, the agent is in a state of intending (now) not to respond, this impulse will be resisted. "Resisting an impulse," at least an impulse of this type, may itself be an act-type in the repertoires of many people. If so, the reason no volition occurred which generated the agent's responding is that *another* volition occurred which prevented it. And the reason this other volition occurred is that the agent was in a state of intending (now) not to respond.

Perhaps the agent felt no impulse to respond. Still, his failure to respond was intentional because he *would* have resisted any such impulse, because he was in a state of intending (now) not to respond. We can regard this as a second way in which his being in this state "explains why" no relevant volition occurred.

Intentionally not doing an A, then, is not doing an A when one's not doing an A can be explained in this fashion, by one's being in a state of intending (now) not to do an A. The latter state is one in which impulses to do an A will be resisted, and, we may add, measures will be taken if the agent believes them necessary to ensure that they will be resisted. For example, the agent may clench his teeth to make it impossible to speak a greeting. He may clench his teeth even before hearing the other's greeting, when he is still in a state of intending to not respond on an occasion which has not quite arrived yet. This underscores the already obvious close connection between intending not to do an A on O and intending (now) not to do an A, hence intentionally not doing an A.

As a final comment on omissions, intentional or otherwise, we may note that they are not actions. Actions are volitions, but an omission is the failure of a volition to occur. This is so even in the case where an agent intentionally refrains from doing an A in part by resisting an impulse to do an A. His resisting the impulse was an action, but despite the word "by" in the preceding sentence, we cannot say that it generated his not doing an A. At best, it generated his preventing himself from doing an A, but this is different.[23]

---

event to occur—and so cannot be an effect. See Bibliography for contrasting views on "negative events," and "negative actions" as well.

[23] An agent's omitting to do an A may generate his doing a B—e.g., he may insult another, and cause him unhappiness, by failing to return a greeting. Still, he has performed no action. Perhaps what we should say is that the agent may bear responsibility for the state of affairs (the nonoccurrence of a greeting in response) which constituted the insult and which explains why the other person experienced unhappiness. Compare Judith J. Thomson, *Acts and Other Events* (Ithaca and London: Cornell University Press, 1977), pp. 212–18.

CHAPTER FIVE

Explanations
of Actions

Often we want to know why an agent did something which he apparently did intentionally. The reply may entail that it was not done intentionally, and even that it was not an action at all. "He turned out the light by mistake, thinking the switch was for the doorbell." "He turned out the light by accident: he fainted, and fell against the switch." We will consider only cases where neither of these is so, and we will concentrate on explanations of actions which give the agent's *reason* for doing it.[1] "He turned out the light because he thought it was unnecessary and wasteful to have it on during the day." Notice that this example, like all "reasons-explanations," as we shall call them, mentions an *antecedent* of the action—in this case, a belief he held which prompted him to the action.

Explanations of actions, and especially reasons-explanations, are called

[1] For some discussion of unintentional and accidental doings, see J. L. Austin, "A Plea for Excuses," *Proceedings of the Aristotelian Society*, 57 (1956–57), 1–30. Note also the contention of R. S. Peters, *The Concept of Motivation* (London: Routledge and Kegan Paul, 1958), that causal explanations are possible only in cases where something has "gone wrong" in action.

for and given in contexts more serious than idle curiosity about our friends. Perhaps the agent is a candidate for a responsible position and his prospective employers want some idea of the factors likely to motivate his behavior in that position. Or he may be on trial for a crime in which it is important to establish his motive. Or our interest may be in *him* only as a specimen of a certain culture, or of humanity in general. We want to know how and why people, or members of a given culture, do act and are capable of acting. In one direction, novelists cater to this more general interest by describing and helping us to understand the actions of persons who do not even exist. Many social and behavioral scientists, especially historians and anthropologists, do this also for actions of persons and groups of persons who did or do exist. But it appears that the social and behavioral sciences aim also at framing *explanatory theories* of behavior. These would enable us to explain actions in ways more formal and rigorous than afforded by novelists, perhaps of greater potential usefulness in applied psychology, in guiding political and economic policy decisions, and so on.

There has been considerable controversy, however, about these theories and the explanations they make possible. Some argue that they are not really "scientific," as their counterparts in physics and chemistry are supposed to be. Others agree that explanations of actions differ radically from explanations of phenomena in the inorganic and even the subhuman world, but deny that the examples of physics, chemistry, and even biology define what is to count as "genuine" explanation and "genuine" science. Still others deny that the difference is radical enough to raise questions of principle.

The issues are too complex for full treatment here. In this chapter we will explore part of the dispute about reasons-explanations and comment more briefly on some of the other kinds of explanations.

EXPLAINING ACTIONS AND EXPLAINING EVENTS   Suppose that Sam stood on his head because he wanted to impress Sue and believed she would be impressed by such a feat. To give this reasons-explanation of his action is to show the action's *point* or *rationale*. We may continue to think the action childish or ill-advised for one reason or another (perhaps we know that Sue is wholly uninterested in gymnastic displays), but knowing his reason, we can understand how the action could have been *justified or appropriate from the agent's point of view,* from the beliefs and objectives with which he started. The explanation renders Sam's action *intelligible* to us. (Note, however, that even Sam may have thought his reason for acting was not good enough, if, for example, his action was against his better judgment.)

None of the italicized words and phrases in the preceding paragraph has application to explanations of events which are not actions. If an airplane crashes, considerable effort is often expended to find out why. Perhaps the explanation is offered that it crashed because a large bird collided with the air-intake, clogging it and preventing air from reaching the jet engine. The collision had neither point nor rationale, nor was it justified or appropriate from the point of view of any of the relevant parties, including the bird.

The explanation of the plane crash in terms of the collision is a *causal* explanation. The collision caused the crash, made it happen; and the explanation which tells us the cause shows us why the crash *had to happen* (for we know a jet plane with clogged air-intake and no extraordinary means of support cannot remain aloft). While the explanation of Sam's action aims at displaying the action's intelligibility, this explanation of the plane crash, a "mere" event, aims at displaying its *inevitability*. Reasons-explanations and causal explanations differ, then, in their aims and the battery of concepts that apply to them.

Closer examination suggests that they also differ in logical structure. Causal explanations have been analyzed as conforming to what is called the "deductive-nomological model of explanation."[2] That is, they show how a statement reporting the occurrence of the event being explained may be *deduced* from a statement describing the cause of the event together with a generalization backed by *causal laws*. (*Nomos* is Greek for "law.") In this example, we noted that a plane with clogged air-intake will fall, other things equal; and this generalization is ultimately a matter of laws of nature implying a need for oxygen if the jet fuel is to explode and generate thrust, and a need for thrust if an unsupported heavier-than-air object is not to take a sharply downward trajectory. This generalization, together with a statement describing the initial conditions, enables us to deduce that a crash occurred:

(1a) A jet plane whose air-intake gets clogged in flight will fall to the ground (other things equal).
(1b) A bird collided with this jet plane in flight, clogging the latter's air-intake (and "other things" were "equal").

(1c) Therefore, the plane fell to the ground—i.e., it crashed.

The fact that (1c) is deducible from (1a) and (1b) explains how the explanation as a whole accomplishes its aim of showing the inevitability of

2 This model is associated mostly with the name of Carl G. Hempel, who discusses it in his *Philosophy of Natural Science* (Englewood Cliffs, N.J.: Prentice-Hall, Inc., 1966), pp. 47–58. See also his *Aspects of Scientific Explanation and Other Essays in the Philosophy of Science* (New York: The Free Press, 1965).

the crash, given the initial conditions and the (causal) laws of nature. For if we know that (1a) and (1b) are true, we know that (1c) *must* also be true. The crash "had to happen."

The explanation of Sam's action exhibits none of this structure, but one that is profoundly different:

(2a) Sam wanted to impress Sue and believed that she would be impressed if he stood on his head.

(2b) So, he stood on his head.

This is neither deductive nor nomological. Statement (2a) indeed describes initial conditions obtaining prior to the action being explained. But no law, causal or otherwise, nor any generalization backed by laws, is cited. The explanation takes us directly from (2a) to (2b), although (2b) does not follow deductively from (2a). There was no necessity, no inevitability, in Sam's acting on his desire and belief. But given that he did act in this way, statement (2a), by giving us his reason, makes the action intelligible to us.

If this comparison of reasons-explanations and causal explanations is sound, it bears out the position of those who see a deep and permanent division between the physical sciences on the one hand, and the social and behavioral sciences on the other. Any science which offers or utilizes reasons-explanations of human behavior is of a radically different character from sciences like physics and chemistry, which presumably seek only causal explanations of the phenomena they deal with. Some say the former are not properly called "sciences" at all. Others say that reasons-explanations are the only proper explanations of the behavior of creatures who do, after all, act for reasons, and so "true" sciences dealing with human behavior will employ them.[3]

REASONS-EXPLANATIONS AS CAUSAL

Against all this it is argued that contrasting (1a–c) and (2a–b) is not a fair comparison of reasons and causal explanations, and that even if there is a difference, or partial difference, in their aims, their logical structure is really the same. In fact, reasons-explanations are just a type of causal explanation. Whatever special features they may have, such as their connection with intelligibility rather than *just* inevitability,

---

[3] For views of these sorts, see Georg Henrik von Wright, *Explanation and Understanding* (Ithaca, N.Y.: Cornell University Press, 1971); Peter Winch, *The Idea of a Social Science and Its Relation to Philosophy* (London: Routledge and Kegan Paul, 1958); and Rom Harré and Paul Secord, *The Explanation of Social Behavior* (Oxford: Basil Blackwell, 1972). Von Wright especially gives a historical discussion and ample bibliography.

stems from their subject matter and our interests in that subject matter. We may note two general strategies followed by those arguing in this way.

First, it may be claimed that (2a–b) is incomplete as it stands. If we find it satisfying, it is only because we are taking for granted an appropriate generalization which if it were supplied, would make explanation (2) just like explanation (1):

(2a′) A person who wants to do an A and believes his doing a B would generate his doing an A will do a B (other things equal).

Recall that in our very first statement of the explanation of the plane crash, we also did not cite a generalization. We merely said the plane crashed "because a large bird collided with the air-intake, clogging it and preventing air from reaching the jet engine." This was also incomplete as it stood, but was acceptable because we all take for granted some such generalization as was finally made explicit in (1a). So both (1) and (2) are equally nomological. To make argument (2) deductive as well, we must bring the wording of (2a′) into greater harmony with (2a), and add to (2a) a clause to the effect that "other things" were "equal," just as we have in (1b). But "other things" *were* "equal"—if they were not, Sam would not have acted as he did—so there is no harm in this. Accordingly, (1) and (2) have precisely the same logical structure.[4]

In reply to this first strategy, it has been argued that (A) generalizations like (2a′) are not backed by causal laws as are the generalizations of genuine causal explanations; (B) the phrase "other things equal" in generalizations like (2a′) is an illegitimate "fudge-factor" which can be removed only by making the generalization trivial; and (C) arguments like (2) as originally presented *are* entirely complete and satisfying whether or not any generalization like (2a′) is taken for granted.

A hint of the reasoning in support of (A) may be gotten from the fact that (2a′) contains a double reference to the act-type B. What (2a′) boils down to is the truism that "people do what they have reason to do (other things equal)," and, it is alleged, this truism is more a matter of *definition* and *logic* than of empirically discovered causal laws of nature. (Compare our functional characterization of a volition to do an A as "likely to occur when [and only when] the agent has reason to do an A.") Nothing like this is true of the generalization (1a), which really is backed by causal laws.

This is a very summary presentation of the celebrated *logical connec-*

4 Carl Hempel takes roughly this strategy. See his "The Function of General Laws in History," *Journal of Philosophy,* XXXIX (1942), 35–48 (reprinted in his *Aspects,* pp. 231–43); and "Rational Action," *Proceedings and Addresses of the American Philosophical Association,* 35 (1961–62), 5–23 (reprinted in Norman S. Care and Charles Landesman, eds., *Readings in the Theory of Action* [Bloomington: Indiana University Press, 1968] pp. 281–305); and see footnote 6 below.

tion argument, which in one form or another has attracted a good many philosophers, but it is ultimately unconvincing.[5] A truism that is "a matter of definition and logic" can *also* be backed by causal laws: "If the switch is turned to the 'off' position, the current will cease (other things equal)." We may not *know* the causal laws on which (2a') ultimately depends, but most of us do not know with any precision the laws on which (1a) depends, and some of us may not know them at all. The very vocabulary of these laws may have nothing in common with the vocabulary of (1a) and be unknown to those of us who have not studied physics or chemistry. Still, we can understand and be informed by the explanation (1). Proponents of the logical connection argument often see another related contrast between reasons-explanations and causal explanations. They deny, or come close to denying, that statements like (2a) really describe antecedents, initial conditions obtaining prior to the action. This suggests they have confused reasons-explanations with another kind of explanation, perhaps one of those discussed later in this chapter.

The reasoning in favor of (B) and (C) is harder to shake off. In (1a), the clause "other things equal" serves only to rule out miraculous improbabilities, such as a super-strong wind enabling the plane to descend gently, or unmentioned factors of obvious relevance, such as the plane's possessing an auxiliary air-intake. In (2a'), the clause serves these functions as well—for example, the agent must believe correctly that he has the ability to do a B. But there is more. The agent must not be "irrational," and must not have "stronger" reason to do something incompatible with doing a B than he has for doing a B. The words in quotation marks are far from clear. But even supposing we understand them, we still do not have enough. A fully rational person with the ability and unrivaled reason to do a B might still fail to do a B; the possibility of such irresolute behavior was mentioned in the preceding chapter. To rule this possibility out, we would have to understand the "other things equal" clause in (2a') as incorporating something like "the agent is a person who *will do a B* when all these other conditions are met." But this would make (2a') completely trivial no matter how numerous and subtle were the "other conditions" taken into consideration. The "explanation" of

---

[5] The literature on this argument and the related claims (B) and (C) is voluminous. An early presentation is in A. I. Melden, *Free Action* (London: Routledge and Kegan Paul, 1961), and the classic response is by Donald Davidson, "Actions, Reasons, and Causes," *Journal of Philosophy,* LX (1963), 685–700 (reprinted in Myles Brand, ed., *The Nature of Human Action* [Glenview, Ill.: Scott, Foresman and Company, 1970], pp. 67–79). Nothing written since seems to overcome Davidson's criticisms. Essentially his criticisms are presented by Jerome Shaffer, *Philosophy of Mind* (Englewood Cliffs, N.J.: Prentice-Hall, Inc., 1968), pp. 97–104. For other references and discussion, see Keith S. Donnellan, "Reasons and Causes," in Paul Edwards, ed., *The Encyclopedia of Philosophy* (New York: Macmillan Publishing Company, 1967), VII, 85–88; and Donald F. Gustafson, "A Critical Survey of the Reasons vs. Causes Arguments in Recent Philosophy of Action," *Metaphilosophy,* 4 (1973), 269–97.

which it is a part would provide only an illusion of understanding why Sam acted as he did, for it depends on the bare assertion that he *would* act this way in the given circumstances.

This reinforces the plausibility of (C). We do not in fact know how to spell out (2a′) or anything similar to get a true generalization of the kind needed for explanations conforming to the deductive-nomological model. Nonetheless, we find the explanation (2) genuinely informative. The generalization is simply irrelevant to the explanation. So reasons-explanations are *not* to be analyzed as conforming to the deductive-nomological model; they differ fundamentally from causal explanations.

There is more to be said on both sides of this debate. But we shall turn now to the second strategy of argument that reasons-explanations are really just one type of causal explanation.[6]

Claims like (B) and (C) have been advanced against the role of generalizations like (1a) in the explanation of "mere" events like the plane crash; that is, it is argued that causal explanations themselves are not to be analyzed in terms of the deductive-nomological model. This is a very controversial subject in philosophy of science. Let us, then, be agnostic and not commit ourselves to any position on the logical structure of causal explanations or the role played by generalizations in them. What we can say with much greater safety is that an explanation citing the collision of plane and bird is a correct causal explanation of the plane crash only if it is true that this collision caused the crash. Similarly, it is claimed, an explanation of Sam's action in terms of his desire to impress Sue and his belief that standing on his head would impress her is a correct reasons-explanation only if the following is true:

(3) This desire and belief caused his action.

Whatever differences there may be between reasons-explanations and (other) causal explanations, they have this much in common. The explanation is correct only if it is in terms of something which caused the event being explained; and to that extent, the explanation is a causal explanation.[7]

---

[6] Another vigorous critic of the applicability of the deductive-nomological model to reasons-explanations is William Dray. See his *Philosophy of History* (Englewood Cliffs, N.J.; Prentice-Hall, Inc., 1964), pp. 4–19; *Laws and Explanation in History* (New York: Oxford University Press, 1957); and "The Historical Explanation of Actions Reconsidered," in Sidney Hook, ed., *Philosophy and History: A Symposium* (New York: New York University Press, 1963), pp. 105–35, reprinted in Patrick Gardiner, ed., *The Philosophy of History* (Oxford: Oxford University Press, 1974), pp. 66–89. Hempel's response to the latter, "Reasons and Covering Laws in Historical Explanation," is also in Hook, pp. 143–63, and in Gardiner, pp. 90–105.

[7] This is Davidson's position in "Actions, Reasons, and Causes." Since we regard causation as a relation between events, (3) would be put more accurately in terms of the *onset* or *acquisition* of the desire or belief; Davidson notes this. (See footnote 10 of Chapter 1.) It is important also to realize that (3), or a more accurate version in terms of "onsets," may be true even if considerable time elapses between onset of the

We shall refer to this view as the *causalist* account of reasons-explanations. The strongest argument for it begins by noting the distinction between the "real" reason why an agent performed some action, and a merely compresent reason—a reason which the agent had, and for which he or some other agent might have done it or something similar, but which does not happen to be the ("real") reason why he did it. Suppose the day before he stood on his head, Sam attended a lecture by a visiting guru in which standing on one's head was strongly advocated as a means of getting a valuable new perspective on things. We know, let us say, that he wanted to impress Sue and believed that she would be impressed if he stood on his head. But is that why he did it? Perhaps the real reason was that he had become curious about the promised "new perspective" and wanted to see if the guru's teaching was sound. Or perhaps neither reason was "really" his reason by itself; he did it at once for both reasons.

How do these three possibilities differ? It is tempting to say that Sam's "real" reason is the one which actually *caused* his action, which actually led him to stand on his head. No more than one of the following can be true:

(3′) Sam's desire to impress Sue, etc., alone caused his action.
(3″) Sam's desire to test the guru's teaching and belief that he could do so by standing on his head alone caused his action.
(3‴) Both desire-and-belief pairs caused his action.

And, the causalist position asserts, an explanation of Sam's action in terms of (just) the desire to impress Sue and associated belief is a correct reasons-explanation only if it is (3′) rather than (3″) or (3‴) which is true. There is no plausible alternative way to distinguish a person's "real" reason from merely compresent ones.

This last statement is more of a challenge than an argument, for we have not shown that there are no plausible alternatives. In what follows, we will present several noncausalist accounts of reasons-explanations. In each case, our final question will be how well the account enables us to make this distinction.

DETERMINISTIC AND	According to those who understand reasons-expla-
NONDETERMINISTIC	nations as causal, and causal explanations as con-
EXPLANATIONS	forming to the deductive-nomological model, rea-

DETERMINISTIC AND NONDETERMINISTIC EXPLANATIONS   According to those who understand reasons-explanations as causal, and causal explanations as conforming to the deductive-nomological model, reasons-explanations treat the actions they explain as

---

desire and belief, and occurrence of the action. For example, the desire and belief may in the first instance have caused Sam to *form the intention* of standing on his head at some unspecified time during a visit with Sue. Compare: an action of lighting a fuse causes a subsequent explosion even if the fuse takes a while to burn, and even though the burning of the fuse is an "intermediate" cause of the explosion.

instances of *exceptionless laws*. Even most causalists who reject the deductive-nomological model agree that reasons-explanations imply the existence of causal laws "covering" the occurrence of the actions explained.[8] We may not know any laws linking Sam's desires and beliefs to the volition or volitions which generated his standing on his head. But if we assert—as causalists say we do assert—that one or more of his desires and an associated belief caused his action, we are committed to believing that there is such a law.[9] Reasons-explanations are *deterministic*, then, implying the inevitability of the actions explained in the light of antecedent events and circumstances and the laws of nature. Given the cause, the action *had* to occur. In fact, many feel that if reasons-explanations were not deterministic in this sense, they could not provide fully satisfying explanations of why actions occur.

In some areas of science, statistical laws are employed, and it is sometimes suggested that an event covered *only* by such a law can also be explained, provided that the event was of a type the law indicates was "probable" in the circumstances. To be sure, the event was not inevitable, but the explanation invoking the statistical law shows there was good reason to anticipate such an event, and perhaps this is enough.[10]

But most noncausalists reject this conception of explanation as deterministic or "at worst" probabilistic. There is such a thing, they maintain, as wholly *nondeterministic* explanation.

---

[8] A contrary view is developed by G. E. M. Anscombe, *Causality and Determination* (Cambridge: Cambridge University Press, 1971). For a critical discussion of Anscombe's position, I am indebted to an English version of Vanda McMurtry, "La Necesidad en el Concepto de la Causación," *Crítica*, VIII (1976), 53–76. See also David Pears, "Rational Explanation of Actions and Psychological Determinism," in Ted Honderich, ed., *Essays on Freedom of Action* (London: Routledge and Kegan Paul, 1973), pp. 107–36.

[9] The law need not contain any reference to desires, beliefs, or volitions *as such*. If mental events and states are identifiable with events and states in the central nervous system, the law would probably be couched in neurophysiological terminology. To get the sort of deduction that proponents of the deductive-nomological model are after, then, *three* things would be needed. The law plus an appropriate description *in physiological terms* of the initial conditions would entail a statement that an event of a certain neurophysiological type occurred in Sam's central nervous system. This would have to be supplemented with such further information about the "initial conditions" and the nature of volitions as would entail that an event of this type occurring in Sam at this time would be, say, a volition to stand on his head. We are not in a position to assemble this further information, but this does not count against this causalist position any more than does our ignorance of the relevant laws of nature. For discussion of some of the details—and problems—of this approach, see Donald Davidson, "Mental Events," in Lawrence Foster and J. W. Swanson, eds., *Experience and Theory* (Amherst: University of Massachusetts Press, 1970), pp. 79–101.

[10] Hempel makes this point briefly in "Reasons and Covering Laws in Historical Explanations," and discusses "probabilistic" or "statistical" explanations in *Philosophy of Natural Science*, pp. 58–60, and "Deductive-Nomological vs. Statistical Explanation," in Herbert Feigl and Grover Maxwell, eds., *Minnesota Studies in the Philosophy of Science* (Minneapolis: University of Minnesota Press, 1962), III, 98–169.

An appealing illustration has recently been provided by Gilbert Harman.[11] Consider a roulette wheel which comes up "red" fifty times in a row. One explanation of why this happened is that the wheel was "fixed" —i.e., it was set up in such a way that it was inevitable, or at least very probable, that this would happen. But another equally respectable explanation, Harman claims, is that it was not fixed, and that "this is one of those times when the improbable occurs." This explanation, if it is one, certainly does not display the event as inevitable or probable; it explicitly affirms that it was *improbable*. Yet it is a possibly correct answer to the question of why it happened, and it conveys information—for example, it rules out the alternative explanation that the wheel was "fixed."

We may think that the motions of a roulette wheel are fully determined by causal laws dealing with the initial force applied to it, coefficients of friction of various of its parts, features of air currents in the room, and perhaps even more obscure parameters such as the velocity of the earth at this latitude and the gravitational attraction of the moon. If so, then we believe there is an underlying deterministic explanation of why the wheel came up "red" fifty times in succession, even if we agree with Harman that "this is one of those times when the improbable occurs" is itself a perfectly good explanation as it stands. Harman argues that a nondeterministic explanation carries no implication or presupposition about the existence of an underlying deterministic explanation. Perhaps the parameters mentioned, or others, fully determined the behavior of the wheel; perhaps its behavior was ultimately random. Either way, the nondeterministic explanation stands.

Against Harman, many will say that this nondeterministic "explanation" is no explanation at all, at least no explanation of *why* the roulette wheel behaved as it did. At best it simply tells the story of what happened, giving us relevant background (it was not "fixed") and reminding us that what happened was indeed a possibility (though improbable) for this kind of object in this kind of situation. As Harman himself says, in this sort of explanation we "explain how we got to wherever it was we got to, without implying that we had to get there." But "storytelling" has been defended as a legitimate form of explanation, for example in history.[12] Perhaps it is "how" explanation (or even "how-possible" explanation) rather than "why" explanation, but noncausalists might say this is precisely their point: reasons-explanations should not be thought

---

[11] Gilbert Harman, *Thought* (Princeton, N.J.: Princeton University Press, 1973). The passages quoted here and later in this discussion are on pp. 52, 33, and 51. Copyright © 1973 by Princeton University Press and reprinted by their permission.

[12] See, for example, Dray, *Philosophy of History*, pp. 8–10, and von Wright, *Explanation and Understanding*, p. 115.

of as "why" explanations, at least not in the sense that causal explanations are. In any case, let us suspend our doubts and see in more detail how reasons-explanations look when viewed as nondeterministic.

REASONS-   Recall Sam's action of standing on his head, and
EXPLANATIONS   the reasons-explanation we gave of it in terms of
AS SIMPLY   his desire to impress Sue. We offered the following
NONDETERMINISTIC   as illustrating its logical structure:

(2a) Sam wanted to impress Sue and believed that she would be impressed if he stood on his head.

(2b) So, he stood on his head.

Like the explanation of the roulette wheel's behavior, this one "tells the story of what happened, giving us relevant background." To complete the parallel, we should understand (2) as containing, implicitly, a reminder "that what happened was indeed a possibility for this kind of object (a person) in this kind of situation (as described by (2a))." Such a reminder might be a generalization:

(2a″) A person who wants to do an A and believes his doing a B would generate his doing an A may do a B.

This generalization obviously resembles (2a′), which some causalists would argue is implicit in (2). But (2a″) has "may" where (2a′) has "will," and needs no "other things equal" clause. The explanation incorporating it or taking it for granted is *nondeterministic*.

But (2) has a feature not matched by anything in the nondeterministic explanation of the roulette wheel's behavior: the word "so" in (2b). This word reflects the fact that (2) displays Sam's action as intelligible, reasonable after a fashion, and we need to understand how (2) manages to do this. Simply comparing it to Harman's nondeterministic explanation of the roulette wheel's behavior—to which the category of "intelligibility" does not even apply—does not help.

A second puzzle. These nondeterministic explanations "tell the story of what happened, giving relevant background." What determines what is relevant? Why is it relevant whether the wheel was "fixed," and not whether it was painted? Why is this desire and belief of Sam's relevant, and not his desire to eat dinner that night or his belief that the earth is round?

The answer seems to be that when we offer what we shall call a "simply" nondeterministic explanation of an object's behavior, we are regarding the object as of a certain *kind*. It is our conception of that kind which determines relevance. We think of a roulette wheel as an artifact that is designed for use in games of pure chance so that all outcomes should be equiprobable, but that in practice is often altered so this is not so. A simply nondeterministic explanation of the roulette wheel's coming up "red" fifty times in a row tells the story of what happened in terms of this conception, so it is relevant that it was not "fixed." We think of persons as beings capable of acting for reasons, though their reasons are not always good and they sometimes act for no reason at all. A simply nondeterministic explanation of Sam's behavior tells the story of what happened in terms of *this* conception. It is relevant, then, that he had a desire and belief which do constitute a reason for the type of action he intentionally performed (and irrelevant that he also believed the earth is round, etc.). Since it is this conception of people which we have in mind when we offer reasons-explanations of their actions, the explanations draw upon such views as we have about what *are* reasons, and good reasons, for actions of various types and display the actions as intelligible in terms of them (cf. the remarks about practical reasoning in the preceding chapter, pages 68–69).

Something very similar could be said by a causalist. Reasons-explanations "tell the story of what happened" in terms of a certain conception of the agent: as a being capable of being caused to act by the beliefs, desires, and other psychological states which give him reason to act. (This, the causalist will say, is precisely what is meant by a "being capable of acting for reasons.") Since it is this conception of people which we have in mind when we offer reasons-explanations of their actions, the explanations "tell the story" of the actions in a way which displays them as both intelligible and inevitable.

Against this, Harman declares that our conception of the agent just is nondeterministic: "We do not believe that certain psychological states must be followed by others. . . . Various moves are possible at any moment."[13] But causalists can agree that the situation described in (2a), say, need not have eventuated in the action described in (2b). Sam might have suffered a heart attack, or been struck by a meteor. Similarly a bomb in the plane with the clogged air-intake might have exploded before the plane had time to crash, preventing the event described in (1c). The question is whether in a case where nothing interfered and "certain psychological states" *were* followed by a volition, we can assert a causal connection between them. A noncausalist expanding on the phrases just quoted from Harman might call our attention to the wording of our functional characterization of volitions: a volition to do an A is "likely to occur

---

[13] Harman, *Thought,* p. 51. Harman is dealing explicitly with reasons for believing something, but it seems evident he intends his account to apply as well to reasons for acting.

when (and only when)" the agent has reason to do an A. "Likely," but not inevitably, nor can the element of uncertainty be removed no matter how successful we are in reducing the vagueness of the characterization.[14] Perhaps so, but the causalist in response can simply point to the rest of our characterization, where we speak of what a volition to do an A "normally causes." Here also, it may be impossible to refine the characterization to the point where the word "normally" or something similar is no longer needed. But the word "causes" is still appropriate. Where the situation is "normal," the relation of volition to what follows *is* causal. Similarly, the causalist will say that when what is "likely" to occur does occur, it is caused to occur by the beliefs, desires, or whatever which make it "likely."

We have been given no convincing reason, then, for regarding (2) as nondeterministic rather than as deterministic and causal. Is there perhaps a reason against so regarding it? If (2) is nondeterministic, what happens to the distinction between Sam's "real" reason for standing on his head and another reason which was merely compresent?

It appears that if (2) is simply nondeterministic, the distinction cannot be drawn. For:

(2a*) Sam wanted to test the guru's teaching and believed that he could do so by standing on his head.

could have been as true as (2a). This desire-and-belief combination gives Sam about as good a reason for standing on his head as the one described by (2a), and we have been given no basis for denying that it was in fact Sam's reason for acting, alone or together with the desire and belief described in (2a). If Sam's action was preceded by some deliberation, the content of that deliberation might provide such a basis. Perhaps he actually thought to himself "I want to test the guru's teaching—but that's a silly reason for standing on my head!" This would be evidence (though not conclusive) that (2a*) does not give Sam's *sole* reason for acting. But it does not rule out the possibility that Sam acted for both reasons; and in any case, such conveniently explicit deliberation does not precede all action.

The best defense of reasons-explanations as simply nondeterministic is just to deny that there *is* a genuine distinction to be drawn between an agent's "real" reasons and merely compresent ones. A distinction can be drawn only between the agent's reasons and mere *rationalizations,* the latter being reasons which occurred to the agent only after he acted or

---

14 Harman especially might argue in this way because he adheres to the view mentioned in earlier chapters that all mental states may be understood in terms of functional characterizations. In the passages just quoted, he is claiming precisely that the relevant functional characterizations must be "nondeterministic."

formed a definite intention to act. But if (2a) and (2a*) were both true before Sam stood on his head, there is no more to be said. A person has reasons for doing something, and reasons for refraining. It may happen that he does it, and it may happen that he refrains. If he does it, then *all* the reasons he had for doing it are equally the reasons why he did it.

If this is not a plausible doctrine, then we have an argument against the account of reasons-explanations as simply nondeterministic.

REASONS-
EXPLANATIONS
AS INTERPRETIVE

Perhaps reasons-explanations are not "simply" nondeterministic, but something else as well, and the agent's "real" reason can be distinguished from merely compresent ones by attending to this extra feature. An important suggestion is that besides telling us the story of actions in terms of our conception of agents, reasons-explanations *interpret* actions by giving us their meaning or significance.

One view taking up this suggestion is that through a correct reasons-explanation, we come to understand the action's meaning or significance to the agent. "Why did you do that?" is a question to which only the agent can give the final answer. The way to determine his real reason is to determine what he himself would give as his most sincere and thoughtful answer to this question.[15] On this view, Sam's inclination (if he can be gotten to speak sincerely) to give one reason for standing on his head rather than the other, or to give both, is what makes it true that his real reason was as he says. This view helps us understand what might otherwise strike us as puzzling, the fact that we generally do accept what an agent says about his reasons for acting. We may suspect insincerity, but not error.

Against this it is objected that sometimes agents *are* honestly mistaken about their reasons for acting. Even if he speaks sincerely, Sam may be deceiving himself when he claims that curiosity about the guru's promise of a new perspective formed no part of his reason. His friends may know better. They may have noted his "accidental" presence a number of times in recent weeks at discussions of oriental religions, his reminiscing the previous day about an old friend who ran off to India some years before in search of Truth, and other bits of behavior strongly suggesting a greater interest in Eastern doctrines and practices than he admits or is aware of having. Coupled with other evidence showing that he really did

[15] Among the many who have expressed views similar to this are Peter Alexander, "Rational Behavior and Psychoanalytic Explanation," *Mind*, 71 (1962), 326–41, and Theodore Mischel, "Psychology and Explanations of Human Behavior," *Philosophy and Phenomenological Research*, 23 (1963), 578–94. Both are reprinted in Care and Landesman, *Readings in the Theory of Action*, pp. 159–78 and 214–73, respectively.

not care about Sue, all this may convince them that desire to try the guru's teaching was his one and only reason for standing on his head.

Supporters of the agent's authority on his "real" reasons would say in reply that Sam's sincere answer can be overruled in this way only if the evidence which convinces his friends could, ultimately, convince Sam himself that he was mistaken. If the pattern evident in his behavior were pointed out to him, he might agree that he acted because of what the guru said (again, assuming there is no difficulty in getting Sam to be sincere and reflective). But if after being presented with this evidence he were still to insist that he was concerned only with impressing Sue, then the claim is that we cannot overrule him. What is *meant* by saying something is an agent's "real" reason for acting is that it is the reason he would give after sincere and thoughtful consideration of all the evidence.

By this reference to the reason the agent "would give," this view of reasons-explanations goes beyond the view of them as "simply" storytelling, telling us what actually happened, and this is one problem with it. Claims about what *would* happen in certain circumstances introduce at least the appearance of necessity and causality (why else "would" it happen?). If here, why not from the beginning, in the relation between the action and its antecedents? A second and third problem are that the notion of "all the evidence" is hopelessly vague, and that no restrictions are placed on the way in which this evidence might be presented to Sam. Anything might count as evidence, if a wild story linking it to his motivation can be concocted; and there may be methods of presentation which could convince anybody of anything! Sam's psychoanalyst, for example, might get Sam to agree that he was strongly disposed to take seriously the words of anybody representing his father, and that the guru indeed represented his father to him, so that his reason for standing on his head really did have more to do with the guru than with Sue. Critics of psychoanalysis might object that Sam's agreement is more the result of a kind of brainwashing than a genuine advance in self-understanding.

A more flexible view takes us back to the account of nondeterministic explanations as "simply" storytelling. The difference now is in what is considered relevant or potentially relevant to the story: not only antecedent psychological states of the agent which we can understand as providing him with reasons for acting, but the whole setting of the action, including other things that preceded, as well as what accompanied and what followed.

The search for the agent's real reason is the search for the *best* story to be told of this kind. We look for an account of his action which will fit into a coherent picture of the agent's past and subsequent behavior. What the agent says about why he did it is relevant in this sense. If Sam says he was concerned only with impressing Sue, then a claim that this was not in fact his real reason would make our picture less coherent, for Sam's words do not fit. This already explains why we "generally" accept an agent's judgment as authoritative. But if there is conflicting evidence as in our example, we may decide that overall, the most coherent story requires us to disregard his words, perhaps explaining them away as "self-deception" or "rationalization." On this view even more than on the preceding, a reasons-explanation provides an interpretation of the action, defining the way in which it is to be seen in the light of its context and place in the life of the agent.

A problem with this more flexible view is that it is *too* flexible. Instead of the meaning or significance of the action to the agent, we now have its meaning or significance as part of a "best story," in which no limits have been placed on the sorts of things which may appear. We lose the definiteness of the "simply" nondeterministic account. We have no criteria for picking out a single story or type of story as "best," and so it becomes possible that there is no single, correct reasons-explanation of the action. Perhaps a story in the framework of psychoanalytic theory would be perfectly coherent and all-inclusive and would identify interest in the guru as Sam's "real reason." But perhaps a story according weight only to conscious thought and deliberation would be equally coherent and all-inclusive, and would identify the desire to impress Sue as Sam's reason, just as he says. Sam's "coincidental" presence at other discussions of oriental religions, and his reminiscing about old friends, would be just that: coincidence.

Some would say this is no problem, it is rather a virtue of an account of reasons-explanations that it allows for more than one reasons-explanation of an action, equally correct though they give different reasons. Reasons-explanations just *are* highly relative to the particular interests of those constructing and offering the explanations, and there are many equally interesting though quite different stories to be told. But this approach may imply there is no such thing as self-deception or rationalization: an agent could always say he is simply telling a different story, which is no less correct than the one he rejects. If this is so, then we have an argument *against* viewing (2) and reasons-explanations in general as nondeterministic and interpretive.

PURELY INTERPRETIVE EXPLANATIONS   The deterministic (causalist) and nondeterministic accounts of reasons-explanations we have discussed so far agree in at least this: a reasons-explanation relates the action to something antecedent to and distinct from the action—for example, Sam's desire and belief. A number of writers apparently deny this. Instead, reasons-explanations are supposed to be purely interpretive, giving meaning or significance but citing no antecedent at all. Often enough this view is combined with and stems from a view that the desires and beliefs themselves are not genuine antecedents of the action; this latter view was mentioned earlier as bound up with the "logical connection" argument which we briefly considered. But a second source of the view that reasons-explanations are purely interpretive, is that there *are* purely interpretive explanations of actions, and these can be easily confused with reasons-explanations.

A request for an explanation of "why Sam stood on his head" might elicit any or all of the following from observers and commentators:

(a) He wanted to impress Sue.
(b) He was trying to impress Sue.
(c) He was showing off.
(d) He was trying to satisfy a repressed wish for maternal love and attention.
(e) He and Sue were destined to become mutually involved.

Each of these five might have the word "because" prefixed to it, giving it the appearance of a reasons-explanation. But only (a) unambiguously explains the action in terms of Sam's reason for standing on his head. The others differ from one another as well as from (a), so we shall comment separately on each. Two points may be noted at the outset. First, all five might be true; no two of them are incompatible. Second, (b), (c), and (d) are in the form of statements *redescribing* Sam's action. The request was to explain Sam's standing on his head, and the answer is a statement reporting the very same action, but describing it as of a different type. Statement (e) could be paraphrased approximately in this way: "He was taking a first step in what was to become a deep mutual involvement with Sue." This fact indicates the interpretive character of these explanations: to understand the agent's doing an A, we are to realize that he was doing a B.

Statement (b) gives a *purposive* explanation of Sam's standing on his head. Together with the stipulation that Sam stood on his head intentionally, (b) does imply a reasons-explanation of Sam's doing this. But it is important to realize that (b) itself is not a reasons-explanation, and that without this stipulation, (b) would be compatible with the possibility that Sam had *no* reason for standing on his head. Finally, the reasons-explanation that is implied if we make the stipulation is still independent of (a), however natural (and usually harmless) it is to infer a statement like (a) from one like (b).

To say Sam stood on his head intentionally is to say at least that he aimed at standing on his head, as this phrase was analyzed in the preceding chapter. And what statement (b) says is that Sam was aiming at impressing Sue. Putting these together, we can get the implication that Sam stood on his head because he believed he would (or might) impress Sue thereby. This belief does give Sam's reason—or perhaps only part of it— for standing on his head. Notice, however, that all this might be so and (a) might still be false. Sam might not have wanted to impress Sue at all; he might have thought himself obligated to do so instead.

It is hard to imagine Sam standing on his head *unintentionally*. To appreciate the role of this stipulation, let us change the example. Suppose the question had been "Why did Sam round his lips just now?" The answer might be "He was trying to say 'Oh!'" This answer has the same form as (b), and it does not imply that Sam had any awareness that he was rounding his lips. It is plausible to suppose that "saying 'Oh!'" is in Sam's repertoire. Accordingly, his attempt—his aiming at saying "Oh!" —consisted in a volition with "saying 'Oh!'" as its object. No belief about rounding his lips, or what he could accomplish by rounding his lips, played any role, and none may have been present. But if he did not round his lips because of any belief he had about what he could accomplish thereby, he did not round his lips for a reason, and there is no reasons-explanation of his rounding his lips. If there is none at all, then "He was trying to say 'Oh!'"—the parallel to (b)—is certainly not a reasons-explanation.

To be sure, Sam may have had a reason for saying "Oh!" There would then be *a* reason, an explanation, why he rounded his lips. But this would not have been *his* reason for rounding his lips. A reasons-explanation of his saying "Oh!" (or his trying to) would not be a reasons-explanation of his rounding his lips.

Statement (c) "explains" Sam's action by redescribing it as of a type which "needs no explanation." Showing off is just a kind of behavior that people will indulge in from time to time, some more than others, whether or not they have any particular reason for doing so, or for showing off in the particular way that they do. If there are human societies or cultures of which this generalization is not true, and Sam is an undistinguished member of such a group, then (c) would not be an adequate explanation of his behavior. But if Sam does not belong to such a group, (c) might be adequate, though it is not a reasons-explanation. It does not imply that Sam wanted to show off, or that he stood on his head because he believed he would show off thereby. Nor is (c) a purposive explanation: it does not imply that Sam was aiming at showing off. What it does is categorize the action—put it in a class of typical behaviors of members of Sam's group. It gives the social or cultural significance of the action, rather than its significance to the agent or his reasons.

Many writers believe that explanations more or less like (c) are especially characteristic of the social sciences.[16] A student of group behavior might explain an agent's shouting simply by saying "that's how people in this society behave at ball games" or ". . . at political rallies." An anthropologist might explain a certain dance as a ritual performance at a wedding celebration. All would be redescribing the actions, interpreting them, as conforming to certain patterns.

It is worth noting that social *norms* and *conventions* are involved in many of these explanations. In understanding (c) itself as an "adequate" explanation of Sam's behavior, we should bear in mind that there are social contexts in which it would *not* be adequate. (Imagine Sam standing on his head during philosophy class, or at a funeral . . .) But the importance of norms and conventions should not be overemphasized. Sam's showing-off behavior (if that is what it was) may not have been *required* by any norm or convention, nor are patterns of behavior that are typical at ball games, political rallies, and wedding celebrations entirely explicable in terms of them.

The explanation that (d) purports to offer is most likely in the context of psychoanalytic theory: in some sense, Sue represents Sam's mother, who neglected him sorely as a child; and in some sense, his action expresses his wish that her (his mother's) attention and love be attracted back to him. We might say that (d) gives the significance of the action from the perspective of psychoanalytic theory; from the perspective of other theories, it might have a different significance. In form, (d) is a *purposive* explanation like (b), not a reasons-explanation. It is unclear, however, just how it is supposed to be understood. Shall we say that Sam believed Sue *was* his mother, and so was "trying to regain his mother's love" in a quite literal sense? If so, (d) together with the stipulation that Sam stood on his head intentionally implies a reasons-explanation, just as does (b). Alternatively, the woman "represented" his mother in some other sense, and we are only to understand his action *as if* he were trying to regain his mother's love. Why we are to do even this is a complicated question, and various answers have been proposed by both advocates and critics of psychoanalysis. We shall simply note that (d) is unlikely to be or to imply a genuine reasons-explanation according to any of these answers, even if psychoanalytic theory were true.

Statement (e) is certainly not a reasons-explanation. It may seem to be a causal explanation, displaying Sam's action as the effect of whatever it

---

16 See, for example, von Wright, *Explanation and Understanding;* Harré and Secord, *Explanation of Social Behavior;* Winch, *Idea of a Social Science;* and Gardiner, *Philosophy of History.* Also relevant is the notion of a "colligatory concept," discussed by W. H. Walsh in "The Intelligibility of History," *Philosophy,* 17 (1942), 33–35, and in *Philosophy of History: An Introduction* (New York: Harper and Row, Publishers, 1960), pp. 59–64.

is that determines destinies. But it is more plausibly construed as equivalent to the paraphrase we suggested: "He was taking a first step in what was to become. . . ." The idea of "destiny" drops out, and all we have is a redescription of Sam's action in terms of its relation to a *subsequent* event. Statement (e) and its paraphrase give the *historical* significance of the action; they are examples of what Arthur Danto calls "narrative sentences," a kind especially important in historiography.[17] Like statement (c), and like (a) as understood by noncausalists, (e) and its paraphrase "explain" Sam's action by putting it into a story. But with (c), the story is a recurring pattern of behavior and events; with (e) it is the story of what may be a unique episode in Sam's life. With (a), the story is mainly of what led up to Sam's action; with (e), it is of what the action led to. Because of these differences, statements like (e) and its paraphrase are least plausibly offered of all that we have considered as explanations of *why* someone did something. Only if "destiny" is seriously imagined to be a determining factor in the past can (e) be so regarded.

**TELEOLOGICAL
EXPLANATIONS**

Charles Taylor has proposed an account of explanations of actions—apparently including reasons-explanations—as being neither causal nor nondeterministic, but teleological.[18] They may display actions both as intelligible and as inevitable, but most important, they display actions as occurring *because of their suitability* for achieving the *purposes* of their agents.

To appreciate the force of the emphasized phrase, consider the operation of a simple thermostat. Changes occur within it which are suitable for maintenance of a constant temperature. Perhaps each component of a bi-metallic strip alternately expands and contracts at a different rate. As this happens, the strip as a whole alternately curves away from and then back to a contact, opening and then closing again a circuit supplying power to a heating element. But it would be strange to say these internal changes occur *because* of their suitability for maintaining the temperature. Rather, each change in position of the strip is caused by a change in the temperature of its environment. A causal explanation following the deductive-nomological model would relate these changes by means of causal laws about such things as the way metals of different kinds respond to heating and cooling. It is only because of the way the

---

[17] Arthur C. Danto, *Analytical Philosophy of History* (Cambridge: Cambridge University Press, 1965), pp. 141–91.

[18] Taylor discusses teleological explanations in Chapter 1 of his book *The Explanation of Behaviour* (London: Routledge and Kegan Paul, 1964). On pp. 37–39 he makes clear that he regards what we call "reasons-explanations" as being teleological.

strip happens to be placed relative to the heating element and the circuit supplying power to it that these changes have the overall effect that they do. But according to Taylor, reasons-explanations imply that the actions explained really do occur "because of their suitability. . . ," and do not just *happen* to be suitable.

According to Taylor, the difference is that unlike the changes within a thermostat, an action and the agent's reason for performing it constitute an instance of a *teleological law* rather than a causal law. It is not clear how these two types of law are to be described and distinguished. Part of Taylor's discussion suggests that a teleological law might resemble the following:

(TL) Whenever an action of type A is most suitable of all the types in the agent's repertoire for achieving the agent's purpose, an action of type A occurs.

Causal laws and generalizations backed by them are also often represented as having a similar form, such as:

(CL) Whenever the temperature of the bi-metallic strip rises above the temperature for which the thermostat is set, the circuit is interrupted.

In both (TL) and (CL), an event of a certain kind is said to occur "whenever" some antecedent condition is realized. The difference is in the way this antecedent condition is described. In (TL), the description incorporates a reference to the future, what *will* or *would be* achieved if an action of type A occurs. But in (CL), the description is in terms of present and past features of the situation (what is *now* happening to the strip, at what temperature the thermostat *was* set). Now we could interpret (TL) so that it applied to the behavior of the thermostat: let "expansion" and "contraction" of the bi-metallic strip be the two act-types in the thermostat's "repertoire," and assign it the "purpose" of maintaining a constant temperature. It is then true of it that it is always performing an action of the type in its repertoire most suitable for achieving its purpose. But we know that this "teleological aspect" of its behavior has an underlying explanation in terms of causal laws like (CL), and of the way it is placed in its environment. In Taylor's view, this means that its behavior is not really an instance of a teleological law. Applicability of a teleological law means *inapplicability* of any causal laws.[19] In practice it might be

---

[19] Taylor seems to have changed his mind on this. See his "Reply (to Robert Borger)," in R. Borger and F. Cioffi, eds., *Explanation in the Behavioral Sciences* (Cambridge: Cambridge University Press, 1970), pp. 89–95. I learned this, after the text was written, from Jonathan Bennett, *Linguistic Behavior* (Cambridge: Cambridge University Press, 1976), p. 72. Bennett's discussion of Taylor and teleological explanation in general is more sympathetic and thorough than the one presented here.

hard to determine whether a system more complicated than a thermostat was governed by teleological laws or causal laws—a guided missile, for example, or a monkey—but Taylor argues that relevant evidence could be gathered. Be that as it may, the immediate point at issue is not whether a monkey's or our own behavior really is or is not to be explained by appeal to teleological laws, but whether our giving reasons-explanations for monkey or human behavior commits us to the belief that it is.

Three difficulties arise for an affirmative answer. First, agents often do not succeed in performing an action of the type most suitable for their purposes. Sam, for example, may fall on his face rather than stand on his head. Since (TL) already limits our attention to act-types in the agent's repertoire, this difficulty is easily averted by rewriting the end of (TL) to read ". . . a volition to do an A occurs." Taylor himself calls attention to the second difficulty: it is not the *actual* suitability of an action of a given type for accomplishing the agent's purpose which determines performance, but the suitability the agent *believes* it has. Sam's standing on his head may or may not be suitable for impressing Sue, but Sam thinks it is suitable, and that is why the action occurred. We can emend (TL), again, substituting "believed suitability" for "suitability." But as critics have noted, this apparently obliterates the feature of (TL) which made it teleological rather than causal.[20] "Actual suitability" may incorporate a reference to the future, but "believed suitability" is just a matter of the agent's *present* psychological state. Perhaps a better presentation of the contrast Taylor has in mind between teleological and causal laws would show otherwise, but the amended (TL) seems to be just a causal law.

The third difficulty emerges if we ask finally how this account can meet the challenge of distinguishing an agent's "real" reason from a merely compresent one. A person does not have just one purpose throughout his existence, but (TL) refers to "the purpose" the agent has at the time of action without giving us any hint how to determine what it is. Using (TL) alone, we might suppose that the procedure to follow is to look at the agent's action (more accurately: his volition), then to examine his current beliefs to see what he thinks action of this type is most suitable for. But this will not help at all. In our example, it is possible that Sam believes standing on his head is the most suitable thing he can do *both* for the purpose of impressing Sue *and* for the purpose of testing the guru's teaching. Nor can a proponent of Taylor's view claim that this shows that Sam stood on his head for *both* reasons. For it is perfectly possible that Sam also believed standing on his head to be "most suit-

---

[20] See Taylor, *Explanation of Behaviour*, p. 62, and Shaffer, *Philosophy of Mind*, p. 93.

able" for decreasing the amount of blood in his legs; surely we cannot adduce this as a third "reason why" he stood on his head!

To avoid this result, a proponent of Taylor's view must supply us with an independent way of telling just what an agent's purposes are. In the preceding chapter and in the discussion of purposive explanation in this chapter, we understood an agent's having a certain purpose as his aiming at something. As the latter concept was analyzed, Sam was aiming at impressing Sue rather than at decreasing the amount of blood in his legs if his belief relating "standing on one's head" to the former, but not his belief relating it to the latter, was connected in the right way to the volition or volitions which generated his standing on his head. Whatever be said about this way, if we now try to reformulate the teleological law in the light of which Taylor would have us explain Sam's behavior, we get:

(TL′) Whenever an agent believes that an action of type A would be most suitable of all the types in his repertoire for doing a B, and this belief is connected in the right way to a volition to do an A, then (his purpose is to do a B and) a volition to do an A occurs.

But the belief is "connected . . . to a volition to do an A" only if there *is* a volition to do an A; that is, only if one has occurred. This means that (TL′) is a mere tautology—roughly of the form "If P and Q, then P"—and not a teleological law of explanatory value.

Proponents of Taylor's view may reject our understanding of "purposive" in terms of our technical notion of "aiming at." But the only alternative in sight is to understand an agent's having a certain purpose as the agent's being in a certain state antecedent to and distinct from any action *for* that purpose. This would make having a purpose comparable to wanting or intending to do something. For example, we might have been able to determine before Sam acted that he wanted both to impress Sue and to test the guru's teaching, but did not care at all about decreasing the amount of blood in his legs. On this understanding, the teleological law (TL) may be restated:

(TL″) Whenever the agent has purpose P and believes that an action of type A would be most suitable of all the types in his repertoire for achieving P, a volition to do an A occurs.

No matter how the idea of "having purpose P" is further elaborated, if (TL″) is to be neither tautologous nor false it will be necessary to add an "other things equal" clause. But even without it, and certainly with it, (TL″) is indistinguishable in form from causal laws and from generalizations backed by them such as (2a′).

The idea underlying Taylor's view is that since people are purposive beings, the explanation of their behavior must appeal to laws of a fundamentally different kind from those used in explaining the behavior of non-purposive things. But if our presentation has been fair, he has failed to provide a coherent account of such fundamentally differing laws or the "teleological explanations" that appeal to them. The truth seems to be that purposive explanations (like (b) in the preceding section) do not appeal to causal laws. But this is because being purely interpretive, they appeal to *no* laws. As for reasons-explanations, we have not yet met with a convincing account of them as other than causal.

CONCLUSION   If reasons-explanations are indeed just a species of causal explanation, then the social and behavioral sciences insofar as they offer them are or can be as "genuine" as physics and chemistry. Whatever our judgment on the adequacy, on other grounds, of theories and explanations offered by these sciences, the basic character of these explanations is the same as in the natural sciences. For that matter, reasons-explanations given by lawyers, novelists, and agents themselves of why they acted as they did are also causal explanations. They may often be mistaken, biased, based on insufficient evidence, or in some sense vaguer than explanations given in science, but they are of the same type. The conception of many causalists may be correct, that there is only one fundamental type of explanation of why something happened, whatever its subject matter, inside or outside of science.[21]

---

[21] This is not to imply any judgment, positive or negative, on the scientific respectability of nondeterministic or purely interpretive explanations; for explanations of these types are not explanations of why something happened.

CHAPTER SIX

Autonomy and Responsibility

If reasons-explanations are causal, then insofar as we act for reasons, our behavior is *caused*. Insofar as we do not act for reasons, but from unthinking impulse, habit, or whatever, our behavior probably also has its causes. But this means our every action may be *deterministically explained,* displayed as inevitable in the light of laws of nature and prior events. ("Prior events" in this chapter includes prior states and conditions.) Our saying that an action of a certain type A was "inevitable" means no more than that a statement to the effect that it would occur and be of type A is *deducible* from statements describing prior events and formulating relevant laws of nature and other information. (Compare the discussions of causal explanations in the preceding chapter, especially footnote 9.) It does not follow that the action was "inevitable" in the fatalistic sense that it could not have been prevented—for example, if something or someone had intervened.[1] Nonetheless, if all our actions

[1] For an examination of fatalistic doctrines and arguments for them, see Steven M. Cahn, *Fate, Logic, and Time* (New Haven: Yale University Press, 1967). Richard Taylor explains and defends a view he calls fatalism in his *Metaphysics,* 2nd ed. (Englewood Cliffs, N.J.: Prentice-Hall, Inc., 1974), pp. 58–71.

are inevitable in the sense of deterministic explainability, then the skepticism brushed off in Chapter 3 has come back to haunt us. Whatever abilities we may have to do other than we in fact do, there is never any possibility of our exercising any except the ones we do exercise, at the precise times we do so. We "can" never do otherwise than we in fact do; we have no genuine "freedom" or "free will."

The threat of this conclusion is undoubtedly a reason for much of the resistance to the view that reasons-explanations are causal. But it is a bit too hastily drawn. Why is it so automatically assumed that determinism —the view that all our actions are deterministically explainable—implies that we have no free will? Of course if the phrase "free will" is *defined* as "capacity for uncaused volitions, volitions not deterministically explainable," then determinism implies that we lack free will. But why should it be defined this way, or any similar way? As one alternative, why not allow that when a person acts for a reason, his action—the volition—is caused by the relevant beliefs, desires, or other such antecedents, but that these antecedents, at least some of them, are uncaused. Sam's standing on his head may have been caused by his desire to impress Sue; but perhaps his having this desire (at this time, as strong as it was, etc.) was wholly uncaused and free.

Usually "determinism" is understood as implying that all such antecedents as well as the volitions themselves are deterministically explainable. In fact, it is often understood as the view that *all* events, period, are deterministically explainable. But with the rise of quantum mechanics in the twentieth century, this view is no longer so popular. There is considerable uncertainty, then, as to precisely what doctrine today's determinists proclaim. We shall have in mind any version of determinism which implies that all volitions and their antecedents are deterministically explainable, even if it is allowed that some other events are not.[2] Even according to the suggestion of the preceding paragraph, determinism would imply that we lack free will. The point of making the suggestion was twofold. First, it is important to notice and understand the difference between these two ways "free will" might be defined. Second, it is even more important to realize it is not obvious which way is the "right" way. Perhaps neither is, and a correct understanding of what "free will" is will reveal that determinism does *not* imply that we lack it.

2 For useful discussions of determinism, see Alvin I. Goldman, *A Theory of Human Action* (Englewood Cliffs, N.J.: Prentice-Hall, Inc., 1970; Princeton Paperback, 1976), p. 172 (hereafter referred to as *THA*); Wesley C. Salmon, "Determinism and Indeterminism in Modern Science," in Joel Feinberg, ed., *Reason and Responsibility*, 3rd ed. (Encino, Calif.: Dickenson Publishing Company, Inc., 1975), pp. 351–67; Bernard Berofsky, *Determinism* (Princeton, N.J.: Princeton University Press, 1971); and David Wiggins, "Towards a Reasonable Libertarianism," in Ted Honderich, ed., *Essays on Freedom of Action* (London: Routledge and Kegan Paul, 1973), pp. 31–61.

How is it to be decided what "free will" is? We must consider why it is supposed to matter whether we have it or lack it. There appear to be two main reasons or sets of reasons. First, many people think that an agent is *responsible* for his action only if and to the extent that his action, its antecedents, or he himself is "free." If he is not responsible, then neither praise nor blame, reward nor punishment, can be fully appropriate from a moral point of view or (many would add) from a proper legal point of view. Second, many people think that an agent is an *autonomous being* only if and to the extent that his actions or their antecedents are, or he himself is, "free." Autonomy is held to be valuable for a number of reasons. In some conceptions of the world and the place of human beings in it, autonomy is believed to confer a certain dignity or other special status; more prosaically, it may simply be thought a good thing to be captain of one's soul and master of one's fate.

If we can arrive at a satisfactory understanding of what autonomy and responsibility are, we may understand what free will is. Better yet, we can dispense with the phrase "free will" and ask directly whether determinism implies we are not autonomous, and whether determinism implies we are not responsible. This is the program to be followed in this chapter. We start with a brief survey of some traditional positions and arguments on these questions.

THE STANDARD POSITIONS   The argument with which we opened the chapter illustrates *hard determinism*. According to this view, determinism is true. All human actions and their antecedents are ultimately functions of features of their agents' initial genetic endowments, the surroundings in which they have lived their lives, experiences and accidents they have chanced to have, and so on. As a consequence, the argument continues, we are neither autonomous beings nor responsible for anything we do.

Libertarianism, on the contrary, denies that determinism is true and affirms that we, at least many of us, are autonomous in and responsible for much of what we do. Often libertarians have argued that we know from our own experience that determinism is not true. When I am trying to decide, say, whether to vote Republican or Democratic in a local election, I do not and cannot doubt that the choice is mine to make. I might vote one way, and I might vote the other way. Prior events do not make it inevitable which way I shall vote. This is as certainly true as many of the things we take ourselves to know without hesitation, and so we may be quite confident that in situations like these, our volitions or relevant antecedents are uncaused. But then, they assert, determinism is false.

Both libertarians and hard determinists are *incompatibilists:* they think there is a conflict between determinism on the one hand, and autonomy, responsibility, or both on the other. The debate between advocates of these two positions and older variants has a long history, but as indicated, our main concern in this chapter is with the more basic question of whether the incompatibilism they share is warranted.[3] Opposed to both are the *compatibilists* (also called *reconciliationists)* who say that if we carefully examine what is meant by "determinism," "autonomy," and "responsibility," we will see that there is no real conflict. Strictly speaking, compatibilism takes no stand on the truth of determinism, or whether we are in fact autonomous or responsible. It is simply the assertion that determinism, autonomy, and responsibility are compatible. However, many prominent compatibilists have accepted determinism or been sympathetic to it; the combination of compatibilism with the assertion of determinism is called *soft determinism.*

This chapter will be for the most part a presentation and defense of compatibilism, but incompatibilism will be presented as fairly and completely as possible.

ARGUMENTS FOR   Determinism implies that all actions and their an-
INCOMPATIBILISM   tecedents are deterministically explainable. How is
                          this supposed to imply further that we are neither
autonomous nor responsible? The most common arguments boil down to two. According to one, determinism implies we are *compelled* to act (and to think and to feel) as we do. According to the other, determinism implies we are *not in control* of what we do (think, feel). Either way, we can hardly be considered autonomous or judged responsible for anything we do.

Stated more fully, the first argument notes that if determinism is true, then all actions and their antecedents are inevitable in the light of laws of nature and certain prior events. It is natural to say, then, that our actions and their antecedents are "determined by" these prior events. This in turn is tantamount to saying they are "made to happen" by these prior events. But if an agent's actions and the desires, beliefs, and so on which lead to his actions are made to happen by prior events, the agent is compelled to act, want, believe, and so on as he does.

---

3 One issue on which the older variants diverged is the compatibility of divine fore-knowledge of human actions with human "freedom." For contemporary treatments, see Terence Penelhum, *Religion and Rationality* (New York: Random House, Inc., 1971), pp. 293–302, or Nelson Pike, "Timelessness, Foreknowledge, and Free Will," in his *God and Timelessness* (New York: Shocken Books, 1970), pp. 53–86. It is worth noting that this ancient issue is entirely distinct from the subject of this chapter, since the divine foreknowledge is not supposed to be based on divine knowledge of the laws of nature.

A standard compatibilist response to this argument is to say it rests on a misunderstanding of what laws of nature are. Despite the naturalness of saying that deterministically explainable events are "determined by" or "made to happen by" prior events, strictly the relation is only one of deducibility among statements describing the events and formulating the laws. And these laws only *describe* the ways in which things happen, the regularities which do exist in the world. They are not like formulations of human laws, which *pre*scribe the ways in which things *are to* happen, and in which force may be used to *insure* they will happen. Talk of "compulsion" is appropriate only in the latter case. A proton does not compel a nearby electron to accelerate toward it, nor does the earth compel an unsupported rock to fall. The universe and its contents just do behave in accordance with the regularities we try to describe in formulating the laws of nature.

Unfortunately for this response, it is not clear that the "mere regularity" view of laws of nature on which it rests is itself correct. Many have argued that laws of nature must be understood in terms of a concept of "natural necessity," and this again opens up the question whether the prior events by which some event is determined can be said to have "made" that event happen. If they did make the event happen, and the event is an action or an antecedent like the acquisition of a strong desire, then perhaps we must admit after all that the agent is compelled to act or compelled to have that strong desire.

A better response is to question this last transition. Whatever "natural necessity" may come to, and whatever may be meant by saying an event is "made to happen" by prior events, we speak of a person's being "compelled" only when he is forced to do or undergo something *regardless of how he feels about it*. We cannot say then that agents are compelled to act as they do merely on the grounds that their actions occur by "natural necessity," given what preceded them. For "what preceded them" includes how they felt about acting in the various ways they believed open to them, and "natural necessity" may very well have dictated that they act in accordance with, rather than regardless of, how they felt about it. Similarly, the mere truth of determinism would not imply that a person ever acquires a strong desire in a case where he already feels he ought not to acquire such a desire.

The second argument for incompatibilism recognizes that an agent's actions are often determined by antecedents of sorts we have mentioned— desires, beliefs, and so on—but fastens on the fact that these antecedents are not also determined by features of the agent's psychology. To some extent they may be. At an extreme, Aristotle believed that an agent's character, which we may take as including or determining the agent's current desires and some of his beliefs, is itself the product of decisions made and actions performed in the agent's youth.[4] But we cannot say the same of the earliest decisions and actions in the agent's life. Yet determinism implies that these also were determined by events prior to them—perhaps the event by which the agent acquired his genetic constitution, or by which his parents made certain key (or trivial!) decisions about how they would treat him after he was born. These events are certainly outside the agent's control. On a view less extreme than Aristotle's, we need not go so far to trace an action and its antecedents back to events outside the agent's control. We do not control what we see when we open our eyes, and what we see may lead to desires and beliefs which determine our actions. One way or another, then, determinism implies that our every action is the inevitable result, ultimately, of things outside our control. But if something is outside our control, its inevitable consequences are also outside our control, whatever illusions to the contrary we may have.

The weak point in this argument for incompatibilism comes in this last sentence. Whatever exactly is meant by something's being "inside" or "outside the agent's control," it seems clear enough that events occurring before his birth are "outside." But before we can accept this principle about the inevitable consequences of events outside an agent's control, we need to be given a more precise account of this notion. Otherwise we can rebut the argument by saying that an inevitable consequence of some agents' heredities and environments is that they grow up to be "in" control of themselves and what they do!

An agent in control of his actions is an autonomous agent. Rather than argue further on behalf of incompatibilists that such an agent is impossible if determinism is true, we will in the next sections develop a compatibilist account of autonomy that will allow us to rebut the above argument in the way just described. We will then examine some reasons why an incompatibilist might find this account unsatisfactory. Finally we will turn to the question of responsibility and determinism.

**AUTONOMY
AND FREEDOM**
The compatibilist tradition has dealt with "freedom" rather than with what we are calling "autonomy," and we should form some idea how the two are related. The seminal idea of the tradition is that freedom is essentially *doing what one wants*.[5] Freedom is a matter of degree, and is

4 Aristotle, *Nicomachean Ethics*, bk. III, chap. 5.

5 In this section I am especially indebted to Wright Neely, "'Freedom and Desire," *Philosophical Review*, LXXXIII (1974), 32–54. Classic representatives of the compatibilist tradition include Thomas Hobbes, "Of the Liberty of Subjects," *Leviathan*, chap. 21 (first published in 1651); David Hume, "Of Liberty and Necessity," *An Inquiry Concerning Human Understanding*, sec. 8 (first published in 1748); and John Stuart Mill, "On the Freedom of the Will," *An Examination of Sir William Hamilton's Philosophy*, chap. 26 (first published in 1867).

not threatened by determinist claims. A person in chains has little freedom; one in a crowded subway has somewhat more; and one at leisure in his own back yard is freer still, other things equal. The alleged fact that their actions (and antecedents of their actions) are determined—ultimately by things outside their control—is irrelevant to this assessment of their freedom.

On this simple account, however, a slave happy to be a slave would be free, since he is doing what he wants, and a dissatisfied slave could increase his freedom by getting rid of his unsatisfied desires as well as by finding means of satisfying them. We may say instead, then, that a person is free to the extent that he is able to do whatever he might want to do. But this would still wrongly classify as "free" the *legally* freed slave so habituated over the years to doing all and only what he is ordered to do that he cannot want (much) on his own.

The phrase "doing what one wants" is oversimplified in another respect. As has been repeatedly urged in this book, wanting must be distinguished from other antecedents like intending and believing one ought to do something. And actions exemplifying habit, impulse, and spontaneous emotional response may have no antecedents of these latter sorts at all. An agent who does what he intends or what he thinks he ought to do may not be "doing what he wants," but may not be less free because of it. Similarly, an agent who bites his nails from habit, waves on sudden impulse, or applauds spontaneously in appreciation is not automatically less free—especially if he has no objection to behaving in these ways. (Bear in mind that not wanting to do something is not the same as wanting to not do it.)

These and other complexities show that a complete account of freedom must attend to internal factors in the agent's psychology as well as such externals as chains, subways, and abilities in general. Autonomy—the agent's control over his own actions—is roughly this internal side of freedom. As we shall see, its possession is compatible with determinism, and it is, generally speaking, a desirable thing to possess.

We cannot deal with *all* the complexities. To get a first approximation, let us adopt the term "motivation" to include all of a person's (a) desires to perform actions of certain kinds, (b) intentions, and (c) principles and beliefs about what he ought to do and what is desirable or what is preferable to something else. Commitments are included in (b); a judgment, say, that one might as well take a second helping and start one's diet tomorrow would be included in (c). A sudden impulse not itself a genuine desire is not part of a person's motivation, nor are emotions, habits, or beliefs not included in (c). An agent's pleasure at a concert does not fall into any of these categories even if it leads to applauding. If a desire or intention to applaud intervenes between the pleasure and the applauding, then that desire or intention is included in the agent's motivation; the pleasure is not. Similarly, a process of deliberation or choice, as distinct from an intention in which it culminates, is not included. Otherwise, the categories should be interpreted broadly, as covering all antecedents of action.

Elements of an agent's motivation may conflict with each other. Ignoring this for the present, we say:

(1) An agent is autonomous to the extent that:
    (i) he does not will (or fail to will) contrary to his motivation;
    (ii) if his motivation were significantly different, he still would not will (or fail to will) contrary to it; and
    (iii) there are imaginable circumstances in which his motivation would be significantly different.

The phrase "to the extent" is vague and we will not try to make it more precise. That is, nothing will be said about how exactly "autonomy" is to be measured, or whether it can be.

Clause (i) captures the idea of "doing what one wants," but in a way which makes it clear that "unmotivated" actions (from habit, impulse, etc.) do not detract from a person's autonomy unless they are contrary to his motivation. An ideally autonomous agent would either not have such contrary habits and so on, or would always manage to prevent their manifestation. (At the other extreme, a pathologically nonautonomous individual might regularly behave in ways he strongly disapproves, each time the "victim of an irresistible impulse.") But an ideally autonomous agent might still often act from habit or on impulse; it is not required for autonomy that the agent sit in judgment, as it were, on his every volition before it occurs.

Clause (i) also presupposes that the agent *has* some motivation, and a repertoire which includes at least one act-type (ignoring the improbable case of an agent whose sole motivation is not to do anything and who never wills anything contrary to this since there is nothing in his repertoire). This is also part of the idea that a free agent *does* as he wants. But (i) speaks of willing, volition, rather than of successful action. *Autonomy* is being defined as a feature of the agent's psychological makeup. *Freedom* is more than autonomy, and requires a cooperative environment.

Clause (ii) is a conditional, comparable in some ways to the conditional embedded in the analysis of ability. Just as in a person's having a certain ability there is a "reliable connection" between attempt and success, so in an autonomous agent there is a reliable connection between motivation and volition. Notice that the "happy slave," who is never inclined to do other than he is ordered, can be autonomous so far as (ii) is concerned as well as (i). This is again the contrast between autonomy and freedom, since it might be the case that were the slave's motivation different, and were he to will something at variance with what he had been ordered, he would inevitably fail. If this were the case, it would detract from his freedom, not from his autonomy.

But the slave so habituated to his slavery that he cannot ever be motivated in a significantly different way would not be autonomous: this is part of the intended force of (iii). More generally, (iii) is intended as a main part of the answer to the following sort of challenge: "Granted determinism is compatible with there being an agent who wills in consonance with his motivation and *would* will so even if his motivation were different. But *can* his motivation be different, if determinism is true?" (Compare the objection to conditional analyses of ability discussed in Chapter 3. The solutions can also usefully be compared.) To see how (iii) does answer this challenge and how adequate an answer it is, we need to explore a way of interpreting (iii) more precisely.

As indicated earlier, our use of the term "motivation" is a gross oversimplification. It suggests something unitary, pointing in one direction, so that what is or is not contrary to it can easily and definitely be ascertained. The truth is that the desires, intentions, principles, and beliefs of a single person may conflict with each other in many ways, and we do *not* require for autonomy that they constitute a harmonious, mutually compatible whole. If we did, then nobody would be autonomous, and the concept would have little interest. Instead, we will suggest ways in which motivational conflicts would be resolved in an ideally autonomous agent. Highest priority will be given to judgments of the form "All things considered, I ought to do (or to attempt) an A" or ". . . it would be best for me to do (or to attempt) an A" in cases where the agent makes these judgments without qualification. This affords us a useful way of understanding (iii).

Clause (iii) holds if there are imaginable circumstances in which the agent would change his mind, or would make it up in the first place, about what he ought to do or what would be best for him to do, and if his judgment would then conflict with what he is otherwise motivated to do. This is not the only situation in which (iii) would hold. It would hold also for an agent who made no judgment at all of these forms, but whose desires or intentions were altered. But it is plausible that this situation is actually the case with many or most agents: they would revise even their most deeply held principles if presented with the right kinds and amounts of argument and evidence. At least this is a plausible requirement for autonomy, something we might call the *open-mindedness criterion*. An agent who fails it, who on some issue related to action is completely incapable of adopting a view or changing his view no matter what the evidence and argument, is with respect to that issue not "himself" fully in charge of his own conduct; he is less "auto-nomous." Etymologically, an "autonomous" individual is subject only to laws he gives himself. To develop the metaphor, if a law once given to oneself becomes immune from review, the capacity to legislate for oneself has been diminished. The open-mindedness criterion is, then, the most important way in which (iii) might be satisfied, and we shall not comment on any others.[6]

The open-mindedness criterion, satisfied by many agents, affords us one kind of answer to those who would press the question, "But *can* his motivation be different?" Given this answer, they would retort with the further question, "But *can* it happen in each case, or can it *have* happened, that the agent be presented with the necessary evidence and argument to effect a change?" Presumably the answer is "No" in many cases, on several relevant interpretations of the "can." But for a definition of autonomy as a psychological feature of a person, this does not matter. An agent is autonomous only if his mind is so structured that he has the *capacity* for altering his views upon exposure to argument or evidence. Whether that capacity will or will not be *exercised* in any given way depends upon what arguments or evidence he gets exposed to, and this is not a matter of how his mind is structured.

To round out this first approximation to an account of autonomy, we must say more about the resolution of motivational conflicts in an ideally autonomous agent. What is this priority assigned to the indicated judgments about what one ought to do and what would be best for one to do, and why should they have this priority? What if the agent has made no such judgment and holds no opinion on the matter, but there is still a conflict between what he has decided (and so intends) to do and what he feels he wants to do? What about ordinary conflicts between incompatible desires?

As far as the matter can be pursued here, the following seems in order as a supplement to (1):

(2) A volition v was contrary to its agent's motivation if:

    (i) for some act-type A in the agent's repertoire, v was a volition to do an

---

6 Cf. David P. Gauthier's account of autonomy in his *Practical Reasoning* (Oxford: Oxford University Press, 1963), which provides that the agent be capable not only of acting in accord with what he takes to be good reasons, but also of "determining for himself" what will and what will not be taken to be a good reason for acting. I take for granted that this "determining for oneself" is plausibly explicated by the open-mindedness criterion, and does not incorporate a view of one's thinking processes as not deterministically explainable. See the discussion of rationality below, including footnote 15.

Against all this, it will be objected that a person may hold a view so deeply that it is an inseparable part of "himself," so that inflexibility respecting it is not a defect in autonomy but an enhancement. A full answer to this, and to problems in interpreting the phrase "imaginable circumstances" in clause (iii) of (1), would require us to say more about "good reasons for acting" than can be attempted here.

A and occurred despite the agent's unqualified belief at the time that he ought not to do an A, or that it would be best if he did not do an A, all things considered; or

(ii) the preceding does not hold, but for some act-type A in his repertoire, v was a volition to do an A and occurred despite the agent's intending at the time, without qualification, not to do an A; or

(iii) neither of the preceding holds, but for some act-type A in his repertoire, v was a volition to do an A and occurred despite the agent's wanting at the time not to do an A, or his wanting to do something else he believed incompatible with his doing an A, and the agent did not at the time want more intensely to do an A.

(A parallel analysis can easily be formulated for the nonoccurrence of a volition during a given period to be contrary to the agent's motivation.)

As mentioned above, highest priority goes to the agent's judgment about how he ought to act or how it would be best to act. If he thinks without qualification, say, that he *ought* to give to charity, and actually puts something in the plate when it comes around, then it does not matter if he had decided that he was not going to give this time. More accurately, despite the conflict between his intention and his volition, (2) does not imply that the volition was contrary to his motivation, since it accorded with his belief about what he ought to do. On a deeper level it might be asked whether the volition occurred because of his belief or merely because of something else—fear of ostracism, say, if he did not contribute. It might be said that if the volition occurred merely because of such a fear, its occurrence marks a defect in his autonomy and ought to be classed as contrary to his motivation. This remains a possibility according to (2), which is not formulated as a complete account.

But why should the belief have this priority? To change the example around, if the agent had judged he ought *not* to give, but decided to give anyway and actually gave, (2) implies his volition *was* contrary to his motivation. Why should this be so?

First, we must distinguish between a *genuine* belief, held without qualification, about what one ought to do or what it would be best to do, and a belief to which one merely gives lip service, even sincere lip service. A person might be taught the desirability of, say, visiting a dentist twice a year, and give frequent verbal expression to this principle without ever having even the slightest tendency to think of scheduling an appointment. There is no need to suppose him a hypocrite or anything so nasty. He just does not genuinely hold the belief he thinks he holds.[7] Once the discrepancy is called to his attention, he might realize that he does not

[7] He may, of course, be deceiving himself, a possibility which raises its own set of philosophical problems. For one study of the matter, with references to others, see Herbert Fingarette, *Self-Deception* (New York: Humanities Press, Inc., 1969).

really believe what he had been taught, and cease talking as if he did. Or he might now for the first time really assimilate the belief. If he moves in this second direction, we would expect at last to find him making plans to visit the dentist, assuming he did not believe there were obstacles preventing him from doing so. If he did not, and we still had good reason to believe he genuinely believed he ought to, or that it would be desirable, we should conclude that there is a defect in his autonomy. For part of what it is to genuinely hold a belief of this sort is to believe that the rule of action contained in it does have priority. An agent who believes he ought to see the dentist believes that the imperative "Go to the dentist!" has *authority* over conflicting desires and intentions not supported by beliefs of this and related kinds. If not, words like "ought," "best to do," "preferable," and so on would not be appropriate to express the content of the belief.[8] Clause (i) of (2), then, merely reflects the content of the agent's own opinion on the matter.[9]

An autonomous agent need not always judge his actions as to their desirability or conformity with duty; and in cases where he does not, (2) implies that it is unqualified intentions which have priority over his desires. Here again the reason may be sought in the beliefs of the agent. To want to do an A is in part to think there is something attractive about, something to be said in favor of, doing an A. But intending to do an A is accompanied by belief that one is actually *going to do an A*. An agent who intends to do an A but finds himself refraining or doing something incompatible in accordance with some desire is an agent who finds himself doing something other than what he expected to be doing. However pleasant he may find it in other respects, this cannot add to his feeling that he himself is in charge of his conduct.

Finally, there are cases where the agent neither judges as to what he ought to do nor has formed any particular intention, but has conflicting desires. In these cases, (2) assigns priority to the desire which is most intense. This is just a suggestion which a fuller account might develop or

---

8 R. M. Hare, *Freedom and Reason* (New York: Oxford University Press, 1965), pp. 168–69 and elsewhere, expresses a similar view. (Contrary to Hare, however, I would not say that the word "ought" here is equivalent to "ought *morally*.") The situation becomes much more complicated if there are "qualifications" in the agent's beliefs. See the brief discussion and examples of these below and at the beginning of the final section of this chapter.

9 For more on the "authority" of one's judgments about what one ought to do (or thinks best to do) over conflicting desires and intentions, see Neely, "Freedom and Desire"; Gary Watson, "Free Agency," *Journal of Philosophy*, LXXII (1975), 205–20; Harry G. Frankfurt, "Freedom of the Will and the Concept of a Person," *Journal of Philosophy*, LXVIII (1971), 5–20; and William P. Alston's discussion of "evaluative stances" in his "Self-Intervention and the Structure of Motivation," in Theodore Mischel, ed., *The Self: Philosophical and Psychological Issues* (Oxford: Basil Blackwell, 1977). The case of an agent whose volitions do not accord with these judgments of his is of course one of the standard cases of akrasia, "weakness of will." See Bibliography to Chapter 4.

reject as seems appropriate; for we have not given any content to the idea of the "intensity" of a desire. Presumably, intensity would contrast with what is often called the "strength" of a desire, since the latter is roughly a measure of the tendency of the desire to manifest itself in action, and (2) deals with cases where the most intense desire is *not* manifested in action. A sign of intensity might include disappointment at not acting on the desire, as opposed to regret (which would indicate a principle had been violated, rather than a mere desire); but this and other possibilities will not be explored here.

Clauses (i) and (ii) of (2) speak of the agent's "unqualified" belief and intending "without qualification." The situation is complicated if there are qualifications. The agent may judge that he ought to do an A but might simultaneously judge that it would be best if he did something else; or he might judge that he ought to do an A on grounds of, say, patriotism, and ought not to on grounds of, say, friendship. The conflicting judgments of each pair might both be sincere and genuine; but each qualifies the other, so clause (i) would not apply. It would apply if the agent came to make a higher-order judgment—if either on principle or *ad hoc,* he picked one or the other judgment as the one of the pair by which he *ought* to be guided. Alternatively, he might decide the conflict cannot be resolved except arbitrarily, and simply form an intention to act in accordance with one or the other of the judgments. In this case, clause (ii) applies, and this intention, formed in the light of the conflicting judgments, has priority.

An agent's intending to do an A would not be without qualification if he simultaneously intended to refrain, or to do something he knew was incompatible. If the incompatibility is fully realized yet the agent continues to intend both, the situation borders on pathology. More commonly, an agent will simply make two sets of plans and fail to notice that he cannot carry them both out. If at the time of action he executes his intention to do an A and simply *forgets* that he was also planning to do a B, which however is incompatible, then there is something short of the ideal in his status as an agent, but it is unclear whether this is a defect in autonomy, freedom more broadly conceived, rationality, or simply memory. In any case, (2) leaves the matter open. Since the agent did not intend "without qualification" not to do an A, clause (ii) does not apply.

AUTONOMY
AND TIME

In (1) and (2), we have focused on the relation of the agent's volitions to his motivation. But aspects of the elements in his motivation in relation to one another ˙*over time* are also relevant to autonomy, and should at least be mentioned.

An agent might unfailingly act on his judgments and intentions when they call for immediate action, and so qualify as autonomous by (1) and (2) as interpreted, yet be extremely prone to change his mind for slight reason or no reason, whenever he has reached a judgment or formed an intention for acting some time in the future. And an agent may have stable enough views about how he should act in general, but regularly fail to realize when particular situations he is in are covered by these views. Such indecisiveness and insensitivity may be regarded as defects in the agent's control over his own conduct, defects in his autonomy. The same may hold for failings in his deliberative processes. An agent may regularly fail even to commence deliberating, not noticing when his situation calls for making a choice; he may often be unable to reach a definite conclusion in his deliberating; or he may simply deliberate poorly, reaching decisions not really appropriate in the light of his own preferences and principles and the information available to him.

Worthy of special note is the capacity agents generally have for making (relatively) long-term plans, deciding not only whether, when, and how to attempt achieving their goals and satisfying their desires, but deciding also, to some extent, what desires to have. On a simple level, an agent who simultaneously wants ice cream now and anticipates wanting it later may decide to save it for later. Ideally, he will then cease being preoccupied with thoughts of immediately consuming it; he will have suppressed or wholly eliminated his desire "to eat ice cream now," having opted for his anticipated future desire instead. Less frivolously, agents decide which courses of study to take, whom to marry, in what order to pursue what they deem to be the goods of life. Again ideally, the effect of these decisions is the suppression, modification, or elimination of desires for the things one decides to postpone, seek in altered form, or entirely forego. And to the extent an agent embodies this ideal, he has a dimension of control over his desires, a characteristic which should surely be considered as enhancing his autonomy.[10]

AUTONOMY, MANIPULATION, AND DETERMINISM

Suppose now that someone threatens Sam with bodily harm unless he stands on his head; Sam, alarmed, does so. Can we say he is autonomous? It depends. Suppose he judged that in the circumstances it would be best for him to comply, and acted because of this judgment. His volition was not then contrary to his motivation, so we

[10] See J. D. Mabbott, "Reason and Desire," *Philosophy*, 28 (1953), 113–23; more generally, see John Rawls, *A Theory of Justice* (Cambridge, Mass.: Harvard University Press, 1971), pp. 407–11, and David A. J. Richards, *A Theory of Reasons for Action* (Oxford: Oxford University Press, 1971), pp. 40–41.

have nothing indicating that clause (i) of (1) does not hold. The next question is how he would have acted had he judged he ought not to comply. If he would have stood on his head (i.e., complied) anyway, perhaps from fear, then clause (ii) of (1) does not hold. But perhaps his fear would not have overpowered such a judgment, and the clause does hold. Finally, we ask if circumstances can be imagined in which Sam indeed would have come to the opinion that he ought to resist the threat. Again, the answer may be "Yes," in which case we have no reason for denying that Sam was autonomous, though he in fact was *coerced* to act as he did. Coercion by threat of this sort is compatible with autonomy. Sam might be as ideally autonomous an agent as we can imagine, yet coerced in everything he does.

What coercion impairs is freedom, not autonomy. The latter we said is the "internal" side of freedom, while coercion is "external," a matter of limits placed by the environment (here, the one who threatens) on the agent's options. (More accurately, coercion typically affects the agent's *beliefs* about his options. Sam was coerced because he was made to believe he could not refrain from standing on his head without suffering bodily harm. But this belief may have been false and the threat empty.) Certain types of coercion may *exploit* defects in a person's autonomy. Harry Frankfurt imagines a person so terrified of bee stings that he cannot resist the threat of one no matter what he is ordered to do.[11] Such a person will do as ordered even if he judges without qualification that he ought not to; clause (ii) of (1) fails to hold and he is to that extent not autonomous. But the threat did not *make* him less autonomous.

Other forms of manipulation of one person by another may directly impair autonomy. Many drug addicts, we may suppose, are incapable of resisting their cravings for the drug, or they fail the open-mindedness criterion so far as the desirability of resisting them is concerned. Accordingly, forcing someone to become addicted to some drug (say, by repeatedly injecting the drug into him) renders that person less autonomous.

It is not so clear whether post-hypnotic suggestion impairs autonomy. Typically, a person who acts in accordance with a post-hypnotic suggestion thinks he is acting as he does for adequate reasons. If a hypnotist instructs Sam to open the window five minutes after awakening and Sam does so, he is likely to say he opened the window because, e.g., he found the room too stuffy. If this reason he gives really was his reason for acting, then apparently what the hypnotist has done is strengthen Sam's desire for fresh air. Provided this desire has not been strengthened to

---

11 Harry G. Frankfurt, "Coercion and Moral Responsibility," in Honderich, *Essays on Freedom of Action*, pp. 65–86.

the point of actual irresistibility, no defect in Sam's autonomy seems entailed so far as (1) is concerned. Even if this "reason" is a mere rationalization, there may be no defect. For example, Sam may have had no desire or other reason *not* to open the window, and the hypnotically derived impulse to open it may not have been irresistible. A question might arise if we move beyond (1) to an account of autonomy that would take into consideration complexities like those mentioned in the preceding section. For Sam may think it objectionable that his desire should be strengthened at the mere behest of another. (Why or how he came to be hypnotized is another question.) It may be, then, that the hypnotist has impaired the control over his own desires which a fuller account would imply an ideally autonomous agent would have.

For our main purpose in this chapter, it is not so important to decide whether these and other forms of manipulation constitute infringements of autonomy or even of some other aspect of freedom. What matters now is the very fact that we can raise the issue and discuss it. The idea of making someone into a less autonomous person is intelligible, and we see the sorts of questions that are relevant to deciding whether someone has been made less autonomous. The corollary is that the idea of making someone *more* autonomous is also intelligible. We can imagine psychological changes as a result of which a person is more prone to will in accordance with his motivation than previously, and better able to respond open-mindedly to new ideas and evidence in forming judgments about what is obligatory or desirable. Similarly, a person might develop in the first place as a highly autonomous being, in control of his own actions and even desires. Each of these actions and desires, and the whole course of this person's development, may be fully explainable deterministically, inevitable in the light of laws of nature and prior events. Being autonomous is compatible with having been *caused* to become autonomous; autonomy is compatible with determinism.

Incompatibilists will protest that this is so only for autonomy as characterized by (1) and (2), and fuller accounts along the lines we have sketched. It is not so, they will insist, for an account of autonomy that "really" captures the idea of an agent in control of his actions and desires. Such an account would incorporate the crucial additional requirement, that the occurrence or nonoccurrence of the agent's volitions, or certain of their antecedents, not be determined. But the question must be pressed: what would be *gained* by adding this requirement? Our compatibilist account is already enough to show why autonomy, especially when coupled with other aspects of freedom, is highly regarded. (It should be obvious that the other aspects of freedom—e.g., the possession of a certain ability, or being free from coercion on a certain occasion—are all compatible with determinism.) Whether or not any nonhuman animals possess any degree of autonomy, the potential for it is distinctively human and may plausibly be thought to confer a certain dignity on us. This is especially so insofar as autonomy presupposes the capacity to judge concerning "ought" and "best," and may be possessed in virtue of satisfying the open-mindedness criterion. And once a being has desires, intentions, and the capacity to evaluate its own actions, it is almost always in its interest—desirable from its point of view—that these be related to each other and to its volitions in the ways indicated for autonomous beings. For if coercion and other external sorts of unfreedom are absent, an autonomous being has (other things equal) a significant chance at achieving the things in terms of which its own interest would be defined. And even if subject to limitations of various sorts on what it can do or thinks it can do, an autonomous being can at least have the satisfaction of knowing that it will be charting and following its own course to make the best of its environment—"captain of its soul and master of its fate" within those limits. This satisfaction is itself likely to be an important constituent of the being's overall happiness.[12] Again: what else would an incompatibilist want, and why?

THE ATTRACTIONS OF INDETERMINISM Compatibilists since David Hume have argued that it would actually be a disadvantage to the agent if his actions were not determined. This is because they tend to think the only alternative is that the actions occur randomly. It would be a strange concept of autonomy indeed by which an agent's firmest and most wholehearted intention to tie his shoes, say, had only a random chance of leading to volitions appropriate for shoe-tying! But indeterminism—the denial of determinism—means only that what happens is not inevitable in the light of prior events and laws of nature. Randomness would be just one special case of noninevitability; libertarians (incompatibilists who accept indeterminism) need not be saddled with it. Many physicists believe, for example, that submicroscopic events are not determined; yet macroscopic events entirely constituted of them are so far from being random that many believe they are all determined! These

---

[12] Gerald Dworkin, "Acting Freely," *Nous*, IV (1970), 367–83, mentions the importance of "feeling free." He also offers a concise and useful definition of "acting freely" which approximately covers both autonomy and the external aspects of freedom: "A does X freely if and only if A does X for reasons which he doesn't mind acting from." A person who hands over his wallet to save his life does as he wants to do in those circumstances, but very definitely "minds" having to do so. Similarly, a person who acts to satisfy a desire which he thinks without qualification he ought not to satisfy "minds" acting on it. The former person is coerced; the latter suffers from a defect in his autonomy. But Dworkin's definition does not allow for "unmotivated" (done for *no* reasons) yet "freely performed" actions.

events—or critical ones of them—might not be. G. E. M. Anscombe gives a striking example of this possibility:

Suppose that we have a large glass box full of millions of extremely minute colored particles, and the box is constantly shaken. Study of the box and particles leads to statistical laws, including laws for the random generation of small unit patches of uniform color. Now the box is remarkable for also presenting the following phenomenon: the word "Coca-Cola," formed like a mosaic, can always be read when one looks at one of the sides. It is not always the same shape in the formation of its letters, not always the same size or in the same position, it varies in colors; but there it always is.[13]

The presence of the word "Coca-Cola" at a given time in a certain position, colored a certain way, and so on, may not be deterministically explainable. No description of the arrangement of the particles at any one moment combined with any statement of laws of nature entails any exact description of their arrangement at a subsequent moment, since the relevant laws are all statistical. Perhaps the particles of Anscombe's example are governed by one deterministic law at the *macroscopic* level, to the effect that the word "Coca-Cola" is always visible. But it is easy to vary the example so even this is not so: the word is visible only *most* of the time, and there is no deterministic explanation for its appearance at the times it appears. The point is that an intelligible pattern can be present in phenomena compatibly with indeterminism, and this is all the libertarian needs.

Compatibilists would still complain that if volitions are not determined, then there is no fully reliable connection between these volitions and all that we categorized as the agent's "motivation." However intelligible the sequence of an agent's volitions, if they are not determined, they may on occasion or often be contrary to his motivation. This would impair his autonomy, not improve it! Some libertarians and other incompatibilists might take issue with this charge. Others would explain that in their view, it is not the volitions of the autonomous agent that are supposed to be not determined, but some key elements in the agent's motivation. (Compare the discussion at the beginning of this chapter on defining "free will.") Incompatibilist conceptions of autonomy (and freedom) cannot be dismissed as easily as advocates of these objections have supposed. But we still have our question: what can be said in *favor* of one or another of these conceptions? This is not so much a request for reasons for thinking one of these conceptions applies to some or all people, but rather a request for reasons why it would be good if one did apply. In search of an answer, we will examine several more closely.

1. An important tradition takes human autonomy to be virtually the

13 G. E. M. Anscombe, *Causality and Determination* (Cambridge: Cambridge University Press, 1971), p. 27.

same as human *rationality* as manifested in behavior.[14] These manifestations include the things people do for reasons, and their deliberations—*reasonings*—about what to do and about what they *should* do. This conception of autonomy may be attractive, but it would require indeterminism only if reasons-explanations of actions were not causal, or if reasoning processes were not deterministically explainable. The former view was criticized in the preceding chapter; the latter will be briefly considered here.

Thomas Aquinas wrote:

. . . For reason in contingent matters may follow opposite courses, as we see in dialectical syllogisms and rhetorical arguments. Now particular operations are contingent, and therefore in such matters the judgment of reason may follow opposite courses, and is not determinate to one. And in that man is rational, it is necessary that he have free choice.[15]

Suppose Sam is deliberating whether or not to stand on his head, which we may safely assume is a contingent matter. He considers the pros and cons: He might impress Sue, and find out if the guru is right; on the other hand, it is physically uncomfortable, and he will certainly get his hands dirty. And so on. Apparently, Aquinas's point is that Sam could rationally decide either way. We cannot say of either course that it is *the* most reasonable, the one for which Sam would opt if he were perfectly rational. Yet whatever Sam's decision, it may be explained by reference to the practical reasoning which led to it.

It does not follow, however, that the reasoning process must be viewed as incompatible with determinism. An explanation of Sam's decision

14 In a chapter on "Freedom as Rationality or Virtue," Harald Ofstad, *An Inquiry into the Freedom of Decision* (Oslo: Norwegian Universities Press, 1961), mentions Socrates, Plato, "their followers," Patanjali, Plotinus, and Anselm as having views more or less of this sort, and he gives quotations and references to Aquinas, Descartes, Leibniz, Spinoza, and Kant.

15 Thomas Aquinas, *Summa Theologica*, I., Q. 83, Art. I, as quoted by Ofstad, p. 140. Compare the discussion here with Gilbert Harman, *The Nature of Morality* (New York: Oxford University Press, 1977), p. 129. A related view is that *coming to know* something, or even coming to "genuinely" believe something, cannot be a determined process. See, for example, Stuart Hampshire, *Freedom of the Individual* (London: Chatto and Windus, 1965). Hampshire is criticized by John Watling, "Hampshire on Freedom," in Honderich, *Essays on Freedom of Action*, pp. 17–29. More generally, we may note Arthur Danto's argument that "he who believes [some proposition] is committed to believe that his believing is [causally] explained with reference to whatever makes the belief a true one," and David Wiggins' observation that even "a libertarian ought . . . to be content to allow the world, if it will only do so, to dictate to the free man how the world *is*. Freedom does not consist in the . . . right to go mad without interference or distraction by fact. Alternatives of the kind which the libertarian defines and demands are alternatives in the realm not of theory but of practice." See Arthur C. Danto, *Analytical Philosophy of Action* (Cambridge: Cambridge University Press, 1973), p. 148, and Wiggins, "Towards a Reasonable Libertarianism," p. 34.

which relates the successive steps in his reasoning seems rather to be a shining example of what Gilbert Harman calls a *non*deterministic explanation, discussed in the preceding chapter. We have already noted Harman's view that such explanations are not *in*deterministic, but compatible with underlying deterministic explanations. Rationality may not dictate whether the pros outweigh the cons or not. Even so, Sam's according more weight to the pros may have a deterministic explanation.

Now a nondeterministic explanation is compatible also with indeterminism, the nonexistence of any deterministic explanation for the event in question. And some may think that a nondeterministic explanation of Sam's decision in terms of his reasoning carries an additional implication, that in fact the decision *cannot* be deterministically explained. This implication allegedly comes from the fact that Sam is a genuinely rational being, as opposed to a being or device (a computer, say) which merely behaves as if it were a rational being. If this is right, determinism is incompatible with autonomy conceived as including genuine rationality.

In response, it must be asked what could back up the alleged distinction between genuinely rational beings and others whose behavior—including internal deliberative processes—might be exactly similar. Nothing in the rationality of the behavior or the deliberation; by hypothesis, they might be indistinguishable. But what else could make a being genuinely rational? Perhaps nothing in what actually occurs, but rather in what *might* occur: a genuinely rational being would be one which would react rationally to any conceivable situation in which it might find itself, whereas for any computer, robot, or other being which only *simulated* rationality there would be situations in which its "programming" would break down and its behavior would no longer exhibit a rational pattern.[16] But if the distinction is drawn this way, the evidence of psychological and neurological disabilities suggests that we ourselves are not genuinely rational. And the question would have to be answered, why does it matter whether or not we are genuinely rational in this sense? What, other than a primordial craving for a kind of omnipotence, could make it seem unsatisfactory that we are, as rational beings, merely finite? There may be a response; but it seems that the attractiveness of indeterminism must be located in something other than rationality, even ideal rationality.

2. Perhaps the most straightforward reason for finding indeterminism attractive is that it provides, or seems to provide, a ground for *hope*. "No matter what your genetic endowment, past behavior, or sequence of environmental influences, there is a chance that on the present occasion

---

[16] Cf. Daniel C. Dennett, "Mechanism and Responsibility," in Honderich, *Essays on Freedom of Action*, pp. 170–73.

for action, you will . . ." How one finishes the sentence depends on what one thinks is worth hoping for. A person with a conscience might be happy to learn that it is always possible that he will behave in accordance with its dictates, however great the apparent pressure of contrary inclination. This seems in particular to be the view of C. A. Campbell, a moral libertarian:

> In the situation of moral conflict, then, I (as agent) have before my mind a course of action X, which I believe to be my duty; and also a course of action Y, incompatible with X, which I feel to be that which I most strongly desire. Y is, as it is sometimes expressed, "in the line of least resistance" for me—the course which I am aware I should take if I let my purely desiring nature operate without hindrance. It is the course towards which I am aware that my *character*, as so far formed, naturally inclines me. Now, as actually engaged in this situation, I find that I cannot help believing that I *can* rise to duty and choose X; the "rising to duty" being effected by what is commonly called "effort of will." And I further find, if I ask myself just what it is I am believing when I believe that I "can" rise to duty, that I cannot help believing that it lies with me here and now, quite absolutely, which of the two genuinely open possibilities I adopt; whether, that is, I make the effort of will and choose X, or, on the other hand, let my desiring nature, my character as so far formed, "have its way," and choose Y, the course "in the line of least resistance."[17]

What Campbell calls "rising to duty" or "effort of will" is a kind of self-control, something we might call a volition to get oneself to do an X. (Compare the comment on "resisting an impulse" in our discussion of intentional omissions in Chapter 4.) Campbell is asserting that a volition with this object might occur, and might not occur. Neither the occurrence nor the nonoccurrence of such a volition is inevitable in the light of laws of nature and prior events. This is indeed a ground for hope, perhaps even for pride in being a creature endowed with this ever-present potential for morally proper behavior.

Unfortunately, the ground for hope afforded in these contexts by indeterminism seems equally a ground for trepidation. For if *both* possibilities remain genuinely open in all agents at all times, then even an agent with a highly developed conscience will run a risk, in "situations of moral conflict," of *failing* to "rise to duty." At least, if we accept Campbell's evident position that a person's beliefs about what is his duty are not part of his "desiring nature," his "character as so far formed," then there is no way of guaranteeing that the person will indeed act on those beliefs. This is not to deny that indeterminism, and a conception of autonomy incorporating it, *are* attractive for the reason stated; but

17 C. A. Campbell, "Is 'Freewill' a Pseudo-Problem?" *Mind*, LX (1951), 446–65, 463. Selections from this article, including the passage quoted here, are reprinted in Bernard Berofsky, ed., *Free Will and Determinism* (New York: Harper and Row, Publishers, 1966).

this other side of the coin ought not to be conveniently overlooked. Moreover, it should be noted that there are senses compatible with determinism in which "both possibilities" can be "open"; for example, it may be *epistemically* possible in the situation Campbell describes that he rise to duty and that he fail to rise to duty. (Something is "epistemically possible" if nothing that is *known* rules out its possibility.) This may in fact be all that he is really aware of, and it may afford as much ground for hope and trepidation as would what he calls "genuine" openness of the possibilities.

Another conception of autonomy may be mentioned as parallel to Campbell's, though it reflects a very different outlook on what is worth hoping for. The Epicurean philosophers believed that a wise man will aim at living the most pleasant life possible (understanding this mainly in terms of the absence of pain), and considered it important for each person to know and believe that he could indeed aspire to such a life:

The happy and blessed state belongs not to abundance of riches or dignity of position or any office or power, but to freedom from pain and moderation in feelings and an attitude of mind which imposes the limits ordained by nature.[18]

What herein I think I may affirm is this: traces of [the natures with which we were born], which reason is unable to expel from us, are so exceedingly slight that there is nothing to hinder us from living a life worthy of gods.[19]

This is one reason they were concerned with believing in "free will." They defended this belief by claiming that the material atoms composing us are liable to swerve in their motions on random occasions. But if this swerve gives hope that we may escape patterns of living which have brought us misery, should we not also worry that whatever physical and mental habits we have formed that make for a tranquil life may at any time begin tending in the opposite direction? Indeterminism cannot be an unmixed blessing.

3. Whether or not an agent "rises to duty," and whether or not he starts on the road to bodily and mental well-being, the simple fact on indeterministic conceptions is that a person's "character as so far formed" is never *fully* formed. A point is never reached after which all that follows are the mere reactions of a set psyche to its current circumstances; persons are always developing, never developed.

[An agent's] possible peculiarity as a natural thing among things in nature is that his biography unfolds not only nondeterministically but also intelligibly;

18 Epicurus, fragment from an unidentified source, trans. C. Bailey, in Whitney J. Oates, ed., *The Stoic and Epicurean Philosophers* (New York: The Modern Library, Inc., 1940 [copyright 1940 by Random House, Inc.]), pp. 51–52.

19 Lucretius, *On the Nature of Things*, bk. III, lines 319–22; trans. H. A. J. Munro, in Oates, *Stoic and Epicurean Philosophers*, p. 121.

nondeterministically in that personality and character are never something complete, and need not be the deterministic origin of action; intelligibly in that each new action or episode constitutes a comprehensible phase in the unfolding of the character, a further specification of what the man has by now *become*.[20]

Perhaps it is not any hope as to what we may do or become that makes indeterminism attractive, so much as the fact, if indeterminism is true, that we are still in the process of becoming.

To someone not immediately drawn to descriptions such as this, it is difficult to explain why anyone should be so drawn. Perhaps there is a feeling of being straitjacketed, intolerably limited, if one's character is not "free" at all times to begin unfolding in some wholly unanticipated direction. But life is after all finite; however undetermined the events making up a life may be, there is still only one overall pattern that will be exhibited by the total record after they are all past. And even if determinism is true, it by no means follows that there can be no surprises, no sudden starts in new directions, in the course of a lifetime, as well as continuing and gradual refinement of a pattern established early on. To say that what happens depends on what has happened is not to say that what happens must inevitably *resemble* what has happened. It is worth noting also that this "developing or accumulating biography view of persons"[21] is actually compatible with determinism as we have characterized it. For we said only that it implies all actions and their antecedents are determined. This leaves open the possibility that other events are *not* all determined, and it is imaginable that some of the antecedents of our actions are determined in part by these other undetermined events. For example, the course of a person's deliberation, hence his subsequent intention, may have been decisively affected by a certain thought's happening to occur to him. Occurrence of the thought may in turn have been triggered by some essentially random phenomenon associated with cosmic rays taking place in the person's vicinity. Indeterminism is not after all required for this conception of ourselves.

4. Human beings like to believe that they are unique as a species in some important way (possession of autonomy or of moral beliefs, for example), and it has been suggested that indeterminism would support a belief that they are importantly unique as individuals. Determinism, on the other hand, undermines this view. For if Sam's action was inevitable in the light of prior events and laws of nature, there are features of those prior events and of the action—namely, the features that would be mentioned in statements of the relevant laws—such that *any* person to whom events having those features occurred would perform an action like the one Sam performed.

[20] David Wiggins, "Towards a Reasonable Libertarianism," p. 52.
[21] *Ibid.*, p. 54.

Our propositions, then, imply a denial of individuality. . . . What I have in mind is only this, that what [Sam] did is *explained* . . . by something that is not individual to, or peculiar to, [Sam]. More precisely, it is explained by properties of his, which, no matter who else had them, would issue in an action like his.[22]

If, on the other hand, indeterminism is true, the action (or a critical antecedent) "has not got a general explanation," and so Sam enjoys a certain uniqueness as the author of this action.

This "individuality," as Ted Honderich calls it, remains somewhat obscure, but Honderich expresses the opinion of most incompatibilists in claiming further that belief in it is widespread and indeed fundamental to many things of importance in human interrelations. Specifically, there is a class of emotions and attitudes which are paradigmatically directed at persons rather than inanimate objects: gratitude, admiration, anger, resentment, and self-directed emotions such as guilt and remorse, to name some of the more prominent. Incompatibilists like Honderich argue that none of these emotions or attitudes would ever be in place or even psychologically *possible* if we believed that the actions evoking them and their antecedents are all determined.

If I believe that his action was [determined, and that all its antecedents were], I cannot hold it against him. At best, I can enter into a kind of feigning. So with gratefulness. I can be grateful to a man for a particular action only if some other action was possible.[23]

One likely implication of this would be that the concept of moral responsibility would also be always inapplicable; this will be examined more carefully in the next section. Here, let us consider the argument that these emotions and attitudes depend on one's regarding actions or their antecedents as undetermined.

There are no doubt many arguments on this issue, but it may suffice to look critically at Honderich's own suggestive remarks. Focusing on gratitude, he says:

When we feel it, we feel several things. There is, typically, that satisfaction which derives from a happy event, an event of benefit. . . . Second, gratitude certainly involves . . . that satisfaction which derives from an awareness of the goodwill of another person. . . . Third, when I am grateful for an act, it appears that I take satisfaction from the supposition that the person to whom I feel grateful could have done something else, and did not.[24]

If we believed in determinism, we would not (according to Honderich) be making this supposition, and so would not feel this third satisfaction. But this third satisfaction is an essential component of what we now re-

---

[22] Ted Honderich, "One Determinism," in his *Essays on Freedom of Action,* pp. 210–11.

[23] *Ibid.,* p. 208. Honderich appears to be developing themes suggested in P. F. Strawson, "Freedom and Resentment," *Proceedings of the British Academy,* 48 (1962). See footnote 34 below.

[24] *Ibid.,* p. 212.

gard as feelings of gratitude; if we all became determinists, what we felt thereafter would no longer be quite the same, even if we continued to call it "gratitude."

Let us not question, for now, Honderich's insistence that supposing that "the person could have done something else" means supposing indeterminism. A more serious problem is an apparent conflict between the second and the third satisfactions. How does the recipient of a benefit from another become "aware of the goodwill" of that other? He must regard the other's action as a *sign* of that goodwill. Now if by "goodwill" is meant some feature of what in the preceding sections we called the "motivation" of an agent—perhaps a strong desire to see others made happy—then it is hard to see how an action could be taken as a sign of goodwill, unless it is supposed there is some fairly reliable connection between an agent's actions and motivation. But if the agent "could have done something else," and if this means that the volition which occurred might not have occurred, even if all prior events and all the laws of nature had been the same, then it seems there cannot be *too* reliable a connection between action (i.e., volition) and motivation. To the extent that a grateful beneficiary takes the second satisfaction, he seems bound not to take the third, and vice versa.

Perhaps the best response to this objection would be to admit that the *action* was determined, and that the person who feels gratitude does not suppose otherwise. What is essential to gratitude as Honderich understands it (and claims most of us do) is the supposition that the *presence of the goodwill* was not determined. The agent "could have done something else" in the sense that his motivation might have been significantly different, so that he would have done something else. The threefold satisfaction felt in feeling grateful is for a benefit deriving from another's goodwill, a goodwill which might not have been there.

But *is* this really essential? Against Honderich's analysis, someone might say the only one of the three satisfactions essential to gratitude is the second. I can be grateful even for the unsuccessful attempt of another to secure me some benefit: I take the attempt as a sign he bore me enough goodwill to try. And why should it make a difference to my reaction how certain that goodwill was to be there? True, if I am the regular recipient of another's efforts in my behalf, I may take his goodwill for granted and cease to feel grateful on each occasion. But it does not follow that I would be incapable of feeling grateful on each occasion, still less that it would be out of place for me to do so! To the contrary, it is plausible that I *should* feel grateful, the more so just because the goodwill is so predictably "there."[25]

To say the goodwill is "predictably there" is not the same as saying

[25] Consider in this light the religious practice of rendering thanks each day for the light of the sun.

that its presence is determined, nor is it clear that the one implies the other. If the laws of nature must be understood as involving natural necessity, there might be some regularities not involving this necessity. If the presence of the goodwill is covered by such a regularity, it would be predictable yet not determined.[26] Honderich and others may admit, then, that gratitude can be a proper response even to entirely predictable goodwill, but add that it is a proper response only if it is supposed that the goodwill was not determined, however predictable it may have been.

At this point it becomes hard to say how the argument could fruitfully proceed. What would be evidence in favor of Honderich's position? On the opposing side, it can be pointed out that it is usually epistemically possible, before a benefit is received, that the goodwill is not there. Suppose, for example, that the agent is autonomous and satisfies the open-mindedness criterion. Then however much goodwill he is otherwise inclined to show, there is some imaginable way of convincing him that he ought not to do so, and being autonomous, he will behave in accordance with this judgment. The recipient of the benefit may rarely be certain that the agent has not been so convinced. Any evidence for Honderich's claim, then, that a grateful recipient supposes his benefactor "could have done something else," may be interpretable as evidence simply that it was epistemically possible from the recipient's point of view that the agent might have done something else. In other words, even if Honderich is right in saying he takes satisfaction "from the supposition that the person . . . could have done something else, and did not," this supposition may not after all be incompatible with determinism.

As a final thought in *favor* of Honderich's position, we may note that the opposed analysis treats gratitude as a reaction to another's *goodwill*, whereas this discussion began by locating gratitude in a class of emotions and attitudes directed toward *persons*. At the heart of what Honderich says about "individuality" is the conviction that there is a difference between attending to a person and attending merely to features of that person, even such an internal feature as the content and structure of his motivation. Opponents may argue that this conviction is ultimately without foundation, that there is no such thing as "the person himself," a possible object of attention distinct from all the person's features. But Honderich is not saying that there is. He claims merely that "people" say there is, and that our emotions and attitudes are founded on this conviction, however incoherent it may prove to be on inspection. It is relevant to point out that in the paper from which we have been quoting, Honderich defends hard determinism, not libertarianism.

---

[26] For more on the differences between determinism and predictability, see Goldman, *THA*, pp. 170–96.

Indeterminism, hence conceptions of human autonomy which incorporate it, may be attractive, then, because belief in it is widespread and underlies ways we have of thinking about one another which are deeply embedded in our emotional reactions and attitudes. Whether *this* is so may be mainly a psychological and sociological question; and the fact that so many people have been incompatibilists, have thought there was a conflict between free will and determinism, is powerful evidence that it *is* so. But this evidence is by no means decisive. Many, including the subtlest philosophers, have made one or more of the many confusions in this area: between prescriptive and descriptive laws, nondeterministic and indeterministic phenomena and explanations, epistemic and other kinds of possibility, and others. Even if a thinker betrays none of these confusions in what he *says* on these topics, what he *feels* (and believes it is in place to feel) in reaction to the behavior of others and to his own behavior may stem from quite different conceptions. Or more probably, the beliefs on which our feelings are based are vague and ambiguous at precisely the critical points. It may be impossible to formulate verbally the belief on which a grateful feeling depends any more precisely than by saying "the agent could have done something else"; and this leaves it simply indeterminate whether the "could" expresses what Honderich thinks it does, or expresses a conception compatible with determinism.

We conclude that indeterminism has its attractions, though perhaps not as many or as significant as has been thought. In particular, we have uncovered no decisive reason for adding a requirement to our account of autonomy that the agent's volitions or any of their antecedents be exempt from deterministic explanation. The possible truth of determinism is entirely compatible with the autonomy of human agents.

RESPONSIBILITY   Is determinism also compatible with our status as responsible for many of our actions? Consider first a possible question about the compatibility of our *autonomy* with this status.

An ideally autonomous agent will never even try to do what he thinks without qualification is wrong. If a person does something morally wrong, then, it may be thought that either he did not know it was wrong or there was some defect in his autonomy. In the first case, his ignorance excuses him from responsibility. In the second case, he may plead that he "couldn't help" doing it. It seems then that no one is ever morally responsible for doing something wrong.[27]

27 Socrates believed that no one ever does evil knowingly. This doctrine, called the "Socratic paradox," led to the ancient discussions of akrasia, "weakness of will"; see

This argument embodies several mistakes and confusions. First, what an agent thinks is wrong may differ from what the agent thinks is *morally* wrong. Even where there is no difference, there may be a qualification—for example, what the agent thinks is wrong, hence obligatory to refrain from, may coincide with what he thinks is best.[28] Our account does not say what an ideally autonomous agent will do in such a case. Second, the agent may have been perfectly *able* to refrain from doing it, but suffered from weakness of the will—and the latter may not be enough to release him from responsibility for doing it.

Thus, there is no simple relation between autonomy and responsibility. Rather than trace the various connections, we will put autonomy to one side and turn directly to the nature of responsibility and its relation to determinism.

In one sense of the word, there is clearly no conflict. Anything which causes an event can be labeled "responsible" for it: "tobacco is responsible for many premature deaths"; "the frayed insulation was responsible for the fire." These statements are true, though both the availability of tobacco and the fraying of the insulation are deterministically explainable. But neither the tobacco nor the insulation is *morally* responsible, and it is here that controversy arises.

Saying an agent is morally responsible for something he did implies that he deserves praise (and perhaps a reward) if the action was especially good, and deserves blame (and perhaps punishment) if the action was bad. But under what circumstances can we say this of some agent? Everyone agrees that an agent with a valid excuse is not responsible for what he has done, and so the issue turns on what is and what is not a valid excuse. On one approach, there are just two categories of valid excuses: ignorance and inability. If the agent did not know what he was doing, or was unable to refrain from doing it (or unable to do something else instead), then he is not responsible for doing it and cannot properly be blamed or punished. (Nor should he be praised or rewarded if the action was especially good; but we will limit our attention to cases of bad actions.) If the agent has a valid excuse for doing an A, he is totally relieved of responsibility for having done it. But the question remains whether he bears responsibility for the condition which excuses him.

---

footnote 11 of Chapter 4. In our terms, apart from the points made in the next paragraph, Socrates believed that everyone was autonomous, and in this it seems he was mistaken.

[28] For example: a person may believe torture is *always* morally wrong, yet find himself in a wartime situation where torturing a certain prisoner to extract vitally needed information appears to be the best course of action. I presented this example and one way of understanding the contrast between "right" and "best" in "The Intelligibility of Rule-Utilitarianism," *Philosophical Studies,* 24 (1973), 343–49.

Perhaps he should have realized what he was doing, or perhaps it was his own fault that he was unable to do otherwise, because of something he did previously for which he has no valid excuse.[29] "Inability" must be understood broadly as including many instances of coercion and other situations where the agent may have had the ability (as defined in Chapter 3) to do something else or to refrain, but the ability could not be exercised or simply was not exercised for reasons we judge exculpatory. We may disagree on what reasons are exculpatory—whether, for example, a certain threat was really too great to expect the agent to ignore, or whether a certain illness really did impair the agent's judgment. But incompatibilists wish to understand "inability" so broadly as to include merely having been determined to act as one has acted. If determinism is true, then actions and their antecedents are all inevitable in the light of laws of nature and prior events, and agents are at all times unable to do otherwise than they do. It follows that everyone always has a valid excuse, and we should *never* say of an agent that he is morally responsible for something he has done.

Among incompatibilists arguing in this way, many libertarians find the conclusion so incredible that they see this argument as a disproof of determinism. But hard determinists accept the conclusion and deny that the concept of moral responsibility has application in our world. This position has been taken to support the view of many lawyers, judges, and others concerned with legal punishment, that punitive measures, as opposed to attempts at rehabilitation or at least deterrence of others, are never justified.

Compatibilists deny that "merely having been determined" is automatically "inability to have done otherwise," and so they deny that it is a valid excuse in itself. Everything depends on how the agent was determined. If the prior events which in the light of the laws of nature made his action inevitable included someone threatening him with a gun or giving him a post-hypnotic suggestion, then perhaps he was unable to act in any other fashion and has a valid excuse. (Even this would depend on the details.) But if the relevant prior events include the agent's greed and disregard for the legitimate interests of others, he may have no excuse and be fully blameworthy, even though his action was inevitable in the light of these events and laws of nature.

How is the issue to be resolved? Many discussions have focused on this question of whether the agent "could have done otherwise"—i.e., granting that the agent had the ability to refrain or do something else, what possibilities were there for his *exercising* that ability? But this may be a blind alley. Imagine that the powerful mind reader last mentioned in Chapter

[29] For this approach to excuses, I am indebted to Robert C. Cummins.

4 is on the scene again. Sam is considering some reprehensible deed, decides to do it, and does it. The mind reader was merely an observer—except that *if* Sam had decided *not* to do it, the mind reader would have intervened and *made* him do it. In this situation, there was no possibility that Sam would exercise his ability to do otherwise; the mind reader would not have let it happen. Nonetheless, Sam may be fully responsible and blameworthy for doing it. The mind reader's readiness to intervene, and so the fact that Sam "could not have done otherwise," are simply irrelevant.[30]

It might help to ask why in theory we excuse agents in cases of coercion and the other valid excuses on which we agree; for then we could ask whether the same theory on closer examination would classify "merely having been determined" as a valid excuse. Pursuing this line, compatibilists have argued that we excuse people in types of cases where (generally) it would do no good (or not enough good) to regard them as responsible, as candidates for blame and punishment. It has been suggested, for example, that there is no point in punishing or even in blaming someone who did not know what he was doing (assuming his ignorance was not itself blameworthy). Blame and punishment are techniques we employ in the hope of bringing the attitudes and behavior of others into line with what we judge appropriate; but they are powerless against ignorance. Neither censure nor a jail sentence will make a person less likely to make similar mistakes in the future. But this reasoning does not apply to cases not marked by ignorance or inability. To the contrary, even if determinism is true and perhaps especially if it is true, we have reason to think punishment or blame can make a difference in the future. Therefore, these compatibilist arguments conclude, there is no theoretical reason for excusing an agent merely on the ground that he was determined to act as he did.[31]

These arguments have been heavily criticized on both empirical and conceptual grounds.[32] One set of objections notes the arguments' reliance on a future-oriented, utilitarian view of punishment and blame. This

---

[30] Essentially this argument was first presented by Harry G. Frankfurt, "Alternate Possibilities and Moral Responsibility," *Journal of Philosophy*, 66 (1969), 829–39.

[31] Among the more important presentations of this position are those of Jeremy Bentham, "Cases in Which Punishment Must be Inefficacious," in chap. 13 of his *Principles of Morals and Legislation*, first published in 1789; and Charles L. Stevenson, "Ethical Judgments and Avoidability," *Mind*, 47 (1938) and revised for inclusion in his *Facts and Values* (New Haven: Yale University Press, 1963), pp. 138–52.

[32] See, for example, H. L. A. Hart, "Legal Responsibility and Excuses," in Sidney Hook, ed., *Determinism and Freedom in the Age of Modern Science* (New York: New York University Press, 1961), pp. 95–116 (reprinted in Hart, *Punishment and Responsibility* [Oxford: Oxford University Press, 1968], pp. 28–53); and David Braybrooke, "Professor Stevenson, Voltaire, and the Case of Admiral Byng," *Journal of Philosophy*, LII (1956), 787–96.

sort of view is not universally accepted. In retributivist conceptions, for example, it matters also that the person deserves to be punished or blamed, and it may be thought proper to give him this treatment even if there is no real expectation of good consequences in terms of reformation of his character or deterrence of others. No retributivist will be convinced by the arguments given so far.

Even utilitarians should agree that the question of how agents are to be treated is distinct from the question of whether they are really responsible for what they have done. There is something to the idea of moral responsibility apart from its connections with punishment and other kinds of treatment. Fixing our attention on this other ingredient may shed more light on the bearing of determinism on moral responsibility.

Suppose we know that Sam did something wrong, and we want to know further whether he was morally responsible for doing it. Walking down a rural road, he climbed a fence and helped himself to some fruit growing in an orchard, despite prominent signs advising him to "Keep Out; Private Property." These facts may warrant the local magistrate's holding Sam liable for compensating the owner, and some utilitarians may say on this basis that Sam should be fined or otherwise punished, at least to deter others. But we have no interest now in these matters of treatment. Suppose, say, that Sam is long dead, and we are his biographers. We just want to know whether he was morally responsible for taking the fruit.

Why would we want to know this? A promising answer is that it is relevant to our assessment of him. How [morally] good a person was Sam? He took the fruit, which we agree was a morally bad thing for him to have done. But to what extent does this bad action reflect ill on him as a person? This is what a determination of his moral responsibility will enable us to say.[33]

If Sam *was* morally responsible, then his action does reflect ill on him to some extent. It shows that at this time in his life, he was morally deficient in a certain respect. Some moral flaw in his psychological makeup broke through, as it were, into action. If, on the other hand, Sam had a valid excuse, then no defect in his character can be inferred from his action. Perhaps Sam was a paragon of virtue and took the fruit because he had been given a post-hypnotic command to do so, or for some odd reason could not read the signs and was unaware that trees growing behind fences are likely to be private property. In these cases, Sam's virtue would not have prevented him from doing wrong.

---

[33] For related views, see Richard Brandt, "A Utilitarian Theory of Excuses," *Philosophical Review*, LXXVIII (1969), 337–61; and James D. Wallace, "Excellences and Merit," *Philosophical Review*, LXXXIII (1974), 182–99.

To illustrate, let us oversimplify, and pretend that virtue is simply a matter of *caring enough about doing the right thing*. If Sam was morally responsible for taking the fruit, we can infer that at that time, he did *not* care "enough." A person who cares "enough" does not knowingly take the property of others for his own consumption without any special reason! We shall not try to say very precisely how much is "enough" (or in how many dimensions it is to be measured); but it is the level of concern expected and morally required of everybody.[34] It is *not* expected and required that people care *so* much about doing the right thing that they will resist post-hypnotic commands, or refrain from taking fruit when they are unaware of any reason to think it is private property. This is why (on this oversimplified picture) the excuses mentioned above are valid excuses. (Perhaps if Sam had cared "enough" at an *earlier* time, he would have avoided becoming hypnotized, or would have learned that fenced orchards are private property; but then it is his earlier conduct which betrays his moral flaw, not his action of taking the fruit.)

If Sam did not "care enough" about doing the right thing, it may be because he had no conception at all of "doing the right thing," or a conception so distorted and inadequate that there is no significant point of contact between his moral views and ours (which we are assuming are correct). This would be a moral flaw or deficiency of a kind, but not the kind most clearly related to moral responsibility. To complete our oversimplified picture, we specify that the agent *does* have an adequate conception of right and wrong. Sam knew it was (morally) wrong to take the fruit; he just did not care enough about that. This combination of knowledge with insufficient concern makes Sam less morally good as a person (at that time in his life). To establish that he was morally responsible for taking the fruit is to establish that his action stemmed from just this kind of moral flaw, and so to give us grounds for lowering our assessment of him as a person (again, as he was at that time in his life).

Now let us return to the question of determinism. Suppose it is claimed that Sam has an excuse after all and is not morally responsible for taking the fruit, since determinism is true. Prior events and the laws of nature made it inevitable that the thought of taking some fruit would strike

---

34 An agent may fail to save another at some minor risk to himself because he overestimated the risk and judged he was not really obligated to run it. Someone wishing to judge this agent responsible may claim that had he cared "enough," he would not have been so prone to overestimate possible dangers to himself. This may convey a sense of one of the many ways in which the picture in the text is oversimplified. Another point worthy of note here is that the picture reduces all relevant "cares" to the one about "doing the right thing." But there are others. In particular, there is "goodwill"—the "care" about another person or about persons in general that figured in our discussion of Honderich's views. Strawson, "Freedom and Resentment," argues powerfully that this goodwill and its opposite are of central importance in our moral views.

him at that moment. Similarly, it was inevitable that he did not then care "enough" about doing the right thing, so that the process leading from thought to action would be blocked. Is this a valid excuse?

If our picture of knowledge combined with indifference as the paradigmatic moral shortcoming of responsible wrongdoers is anywhere near correct, then the answer is "No." Determinism may imply a certain inevitability in Sam's possession of this shortcoming at this time, but it does not change the fact that he *had* this shortcoming. And to say he was responsible for his action is just to say that his action manifested a shortcoming of this kind.

"But Sam could not *help* developing the way he developed, to the point that he did not care 'enough' about doing the right thing. It was all inevitable, given his genes, family life, and so on."

This familiar objection invites us to think of Sam as struggling unsuccessfully for years against the inexorable pressures of his heredity and environment. Or perhaps just sliding unawares into moral deficiency, having no insight into the direction in which he was heading. Possibly even, he was born with some constitutional incapacity ever to care "enough" about doing the right thing (though remember that we are confining our attention to cases where the agent is born with the potential for acquiring, and actually acquires, an adequate conception of right and wrong). Suppose we do think of Sam in one of these ways; what follows? At best, he has an excuse for having become morally deficient. Again, this does not change the fact that he did become morally deficient, and was so at the time of his action. We judge him responsible for taking the fruit, not for becoming the sort of person who *would* take the fruit without justification or valid excuse.

It will be urged that this distinction—between responsibility for wrongdoing, and responsibility for having become a person who would do wrong without justification or valid excuse—does not have force. "*Since* Sam was not responsible for the latter, he should not be held responsible for the former, either." Now there is a subtle difference between "holding someone responsible" and "judging that someone is responsible"; in many contexts, the former is tantamount to deciding to treat the person a certain way, e.g., with punishment, while the latter may be nothing more than a prelude to an assessment of the person's moral worth. Perhaps it is true, or often true, that we should not punish a person for having done some wrong without any excuse, on the ground that he is not responsible for having become the sort of person he has become. This is a complicated matter in the theory of punishment. Among other issues, the general aims of punishment and the particular question of justice versus mercy would have to be considered. To these, the details of just how he became this sort of person would be relevant. (*Did* he struggle?

Did he ever regret the way he was developing?) But once again, all this has nothing to do with the fact that he has become this sort of morally substandard person. (If all he did was steal fruit on one occasion when he was hungry, we have no evidence that he is very *far* below standard or that he was below it for any great length of time; but still, if he at that moment had cared "enough," he would not have done even this.)

There is, then, no incompatibility between determinism and moral responsibility, if our oversimplified account of the latter is not misleading.[35] And our argument does not depend on the details of this account. We described the paradigm moral deficiency as insufficient concern with doing the right thing (coupled with adequate knowledge of what the right thing *is*); anyone unhappy with this can substitute a different account, whose central feature we can label "A." To say Sam was morally responsible, then, is to say his action manifested A. Determinism would imply that the presence of A in Sam at this time, and its breaking through into action, were both inevitable. It would remain true that A was indeed present and did indeed break through into action.

This conclusion can be denied only if A somehow incorporates an assertion of indeterminism. Perhaps something like the following: "To say Sam was morally responsible for taking the fruit is to say (among other things) that at the time of action, Sam might have taken it, and he might have refrained, but he went ahead and took it." This sentence is ambiguous, but incompatibilists would have us understand "He might have, and he might not" as meaning that it was not inevitable in the light of prior events and laws of nature (cf. the passage quoted from Campbell, p. 127). But why should this condition be part of an account of moral responsibility?

It does not seem that incompatibilists have come squarely to grips with this question. Perhaps one possibility is the following. Recall the "unfolding biography" conception of persons discussed above as a possible attraction of indeterminism. If "Sam might have taken it, and he might have refrained, but he went ahead and took it," then his life has unfolded in such a way as to contain a morally bad action which on this conception, there was no inevitability that it contain. His life has turned

---

[35] Nor could determinism conflict with *legal* responsibility. It is controversial to what extent a morally acceptable legal system can hold responsible and punish individuals who are not morally responsible for the offenses in question. But the mere truth of determinism could not provide a reason for the legal system *not* to punish persons who *are* morally responsible and whose punishment would be morally permissible. For more on legal responsibility and punishment, see Hart, *Punishment and Responsibility;* Herbert Morris, ed., *Freedom and Responsibility* (Stanford, Calif.: Stanford University Press, 1961); and David A. J. Richards, *The Moral Criticism of the Law* (Encino, Calif., and Belmont, Calif.: Dickenson Publishing Company, Inc., 1977), chaps. 5 and 6.

out to be worse than it might have, morally speaking. Perhaps this, rather than the presence of a moral deficiency manifested by the bad action, is the respect in which our assessment of Sam is lowered when we learn he is responsible for some bad action he performed.

This view we have constructed on behalf of the incompatibilists may explain better why we are concerned with bad *actions* rather than simply with moral deficiencies which can lead to bad actions. (Recall that if Sam never chances on an unguarded fruit tree, if his deficiency never breaks through into action, we may never have occasion to lower our assessment of him.) But it does not offer as satisfying an account of why ignorance and inability are valid excuses: however ignorant Sam may have been that the fruit was private property, his life would still contain a bad action. And this incompatibilist view does not obviously afford any better understanding of the ties between moral responsibility and our ways of treating agents we deem responsible for their actions than does the compatibilist view we have developed.

No compelling reason has surfaced for rejecting compatibilism. Our responsibility for what we do is undermined no more than our autonomy in doing it by the possibility that all we do and undergo is deterministically explainable.

FOR FURTHER READING

The first two sections of the following bibliography include books entirely devoted to theory of action and covering more than one topic within theory of action; some of these are also mentioned in the footnotes. The remaining sections correspond to the chapters of this book and for the most part list books and articles which I have found of interest but which are *not* mentioned in the footnotes.

Fuller bibliographies may be found in several of the anthologies, especially the one by Brand and the one by Binkley, Bronaugh, and Marras.

ANTHOLOGIES AND COLLECTIONS OF ESSAYS BY MORE THAN ONE AUTHOR

BINKLEY, ROBERT, RICHARD BRONAUGH, and AUSONIO MARRAS, eds., *Agent, Action, and Reason.* Toronto: University of Toronto Press, 1971.

BRAND, MYLES, ed., *The Nature of Human Action.* Glenview, Ill.: Scott, Foresman and Company, 1970. The best general anthology.

——— and DOUGLAS WALTON, eds., *Action Theory.* Dordrecht: D. Reidel Publishing Company, 1976. Papers given at the Winnipeg Conference on Action Theory in 1975, adding up to a full survey of the field by a number of the more prominent persons working in it. Advanced students will want to consult it.

CARE, NORMAN S., and CHARLES LANDESMAN, eds., *Readings in the Theory of Action.* Bloomington: Indiana University Press, 1968.

LEHRER, KEITH, ed., *Freedom and Determinism.* New York: Random House, Inc., 1966.

WHITE, ALAN R., ed., *The Philosophy of Action.* Oxford: Oxford University Press, 1968.

WORKS BY INDIVIDUAL AUTHORS

AUNE, BRUCE, *Reason and Action.* Dordrecht: D. Reidel Publishing Company, 1977.

BROWN, D. G., *Action.* Toronto: University of Toronto Press, 1968.

DANTO, ARTHUR C., *Analytical Philosophy of Action*. Cambridge: Cambridge University Press, 1973.

GOLDMAN, ALVIN I., *A Theory of Human Action*. Englewood Cliffs, N.J.: Prentice-Hall, Inc., 1970; Princeton Paperback, 1976. An especially valuable attempt to develop a comprehensive and unified theory.

HAMPSHIRE, STUART, *Thought and Action*. London: Chatto and Windus, 1959.

KENNY, ANTHONY, *Action, Emotion, and Will*. London: Routledge and Kegan Paul, 1963.

MELDEN, A. I., *Free Action*. New York: Humanities Press, Inc., 1961.

PETERS, R. S., *The Concept of Motivation*. London: Routledge and Kegan Paul, 1958.

TAYLOR, CHARLES, *The Explanation of Behaviour*. London: Routledge and Kegan Paul, 1964.

TAYLOR, RICHARD, *Action and Purpose*. Englewood Cliffs, N.J.: Prentice-Hall, Inc., 1966.

THALBERG, IRVING, *Enigmas of Agency*. New York: Humanities Press, Inc., 1972.

VON WRIGHT, G. H., *Explanation and Understanding*. Ithaca, N.Y.: Cornell University Press, 1971.

CHAPTER 1 THE NATURE OF ACTION

Versions of the Volitional Theory

AUNE, BRUCE, "Prichard, Action, and Volition," *Philosophical Studies*, 25 (1974), 117–23.

DANTO, ARTHUR C., *Analytical Philosophy of Action*, chap. 3. Cambridge: Cambridge University Press, 1973.

GOLDMAN, ALVIN I., "The Volitional Theory Revisited," in *Action Theory*, ed. Myles Brand and Douglas Walton. Dordrecht: D. Reidel Publishing Company, 1976.

JAMES, WILLIAM, *The Principles of Psychology*, vol. II, chap. 26.

LOCKE, JOHN, *Essay Concerning Human Understanding*, book II, chap. xxi, secs. 4–5. (First published in 1690.)

McCANN, HUGH, "Trying, Paralysis, and Volition," *Review of Metaphysics*, XXVIII (1975), 423–42.

———, "Volition and Basic Action," *Philosophical Review*, LXXXIII (1974), 451–73.

O'SHAUGHNESSY, BRIAN, "Trying (as the Mental 'Pineal Gland')," *Journal of Philosophy*, LXX (1973), 365–86.

SELLARS, WILFRID, "Volitions Reaffirmed," in Brand and Walton, *Action Theory*.

VESEY, G. N. A., "Volition," *Philosophy*, XXXVI (1961), 352–65. Reprinted in *The Philosophy of Action*, ed. Alan R. White. Oxford: Oxford University Press, 1968.

On the "Functionalist" View of Mental Events and States

ARMSTRONG, DAVID M., *A Materialist Theory of the Mind*. New York: Humanities Press, Inc., 1968. Also presents a volitional theory of action.

DAVIS, LAWRENCE H., "Disembodied Brains," *Australasian Journal of Philosophy*, 52 (1974), 121–32.

HARMAN, GILBERT, *Thought*. Princeton, N.J.: Princeton University Press, 1973. Perhaps the least technical.

PUTNAM, HILARY, "Minds and Machines," in *Minds and Machines*, ed. Alan R. Anderson. Englewood Cliffs, N.J.: Prentice-Hall, Inc., 1964.

ROSENTHAL, DAVID M., ed., *Materialism and the Mind-Body Problem*. Englewood Cliffs, N.J.: Prentice-Hall, Inc., 1971. Especially the papers by H. Putnam, D. K. Lewis, and J. A. Fodor.

SHOEMAKER, SYDNEY, "Functionalism and Qualia," *Philosophical Studies*, 27 (1975), 291–315. Perhaps the most technical.

CHAPTER 2 ACTIONS AND EVENTS

BAIER, ANNETTE, "Intention, Practical Knowledge and Representation," in *Action Theory*, ed. Myles Brand and Douglas Walton. Dordrecht: D. Reidel Publishing Company, 1976. Suggestive comments on generation, mental actions, and actions performed by or otherwise dependent on more than one person.

KIM, JAEGWON, "Events as Property Exemplifications," in Brand and Walton, *Action Theory*. Here and in other papers cited here, Kim develops a theory often regarded as a version of the prolific theory (though Kim disputes this).

LOMBARD, LAWRENCE B., "A Note on Level-Generation and the Time of a Killing," *Philosophical Studies*, 26 (1974), 151–52. Discusses a problem for the prolific theory arising from a difficulty in pinpointing the time at which, or during which, an action occurs.

CHAPTER 3 ABILITY

BAIER, ANNETTE, "The Search for Basic Actions," *American Philosophical Quarterly*, 8 (1971), 161–70.

DAVIDSON, DONALD, "Freedom to Act," in *Essays on Freedom of Action*, ed. Ted Honderich. London: Routledge and Kegan Paul, 1973.

MARTIN, JANE R., "Basic Actions and Simple Actions," *American Philosophical Quarterly*, 9 (1972), 59–68.

THALBERG, IRVING, *Enigmas of Agency*. New York: Humanities Press, Inc., 1972, pp. 115–42.

CHAPTER 4 INTENTION

Practical Reasoning and Related Topics

BRAND, MYLES, and DOUGLAS WALTON, eds., *Action Theory*. Dordrecht: D. Reidel Publishing Company, 1976. Especially papers by R. W. Binkley, H.-N. Castaneda, and W. Sellars.

GAUTHIER, DAVID P., *Practical Reasoning*. Oxford: The Clarendon Press, 1963.

HARMAN, GILBERT, *The Nature of Morality*, chaps. 10–11. New York: Oxford University Press, 1977.

KÖRNER, STEPHEN, ed., *Practical Reason*. New Haven: Yale University Press, 1974.

RICHARDS, DAVID A. J., *A Theory of Reasons for Action*. Oxford: The Clarendon Press, 1971.

SUPPES, PATRICK, "Decision Theory," in *The Encyclopedia of Philosophy*, II, 310–14, ed. Paul Edwards. New York: Macmillan Publishing Company, and The Free Press, 1967.

TAYLOR, RICHARD, *Action and Purpose*, pp. 167–84. Englewood Cliffs, N.J.: Prentice-Hall, Inc., 1966. On deliberation.

"Negative Events" and "Negative Actions"

BRAND, MYLES, "The Language of Not Doing," *American Philosophical Quarterly*, 8 (1971), 45–53.

DANTO, ARTHUR C., *Analytical Philosophy of Action*, pp. 95, 96, 164–81. Cambridge: Cambridge University Press, 1973.

D'ARCY, ERIC, *Human Acts*, pp. 41–44. Oxford: The Clarendon Press, 1963.

GOLDMAN, ALVIN I., *A Theory of Human Action*, pp. 47–48. Englewood Cliffs, N.J.: Prentice-Hall, Inc., 1970.

Other Topics

AUDI, ROBERT, "Intending," *Journal of Philosophy*, LXX (1973), 387–403. Defends an account of intending in terms of wanting and believing. Many references to the literature.

———, "Weakness of Will and Practical Judgment," *Nous*, forthcoming.

BEARDSLEY, MONROE C., "Intending," in *Values and Morals: Essays in Honor of William Frankena, Charles Stevenson, and Richard Brandt*, ed. Alvin I. Goldman and Jaegwon Kim. Dordrecht: D. Reidel Publishing Company, 1978.

BENNETT, JONATHAN, *Linguistic Behaviour*. Cambridge: Cambridge University Press, 1976. Develops ideas of Grice and others on intentions in speaking. Has good bibliography on this topic.

DAVIDSON, DONALD, "Intending," in *Philosophy of History and Action: Papers Presented at the First Jerusalem Philosophical Encounter*, ed. Yirmiahu Yovel. Dordrecht: D. Reidel Publishing Company; Jerusalem: The Magnes Press, The

Hebrew University, 1978. Compares intending to do something with judging in a special way that it is desirable to do it.

DONNELLAN, KEITH S., "Knowing What I Am Doing," *Journal of Philosophy*, LX (1963), 401–9.

GOLDMAN, ALVIN I., *A Theory of Human Action*, pp. 49–63, 76–80, 103–4, 176–77, and 193–94. Englewood Cliffs, N.J.: Prentice-Hall, Inc., 1970. Identifies intending, wanting, and having a reason.

GRICE, H. P., "Meaning," *Philosophical Review*, LXVI (1957), 377–88. An account of linguistic meaning in terms of intentions speakers allegedly have. (The question whether these intentions really can be attributed to speakers needs to be studied in the light of our accounts of acting intentionally and intending.)

HART, H. L. A., and STUART HAMPSHIRE, "Decision, Intention, and Certainty," *Mind*, LXVII (1958), 1–12. Emphasizes the agent's knowledge and its nonobservational character.

KENNY, ANTHONY, "Intention and Purpose in Law," in *Essays in Legal Philosophy*, ed. Robert S. Summers. Berkeley: University of California Press, 1968.

MORTIMORE, G. W., ed., *Weakness of Will*. London: Macmillan, 1971. Some ancient and modern discussions.

TAYLOR, CHARLES, *The Explanation of Behaviour*, pp. 54–71. London: Routledge and Kegan Paul, 1964. Emphasizes what in this chapter is called "aiming at."

CHAPTER 5   EXPLANATIONS OF ACTIONS

GOLDMAN, ALVIN I., *A Theory of Human Action*, pp. 126–69. Englewood Cliffs, N.J.: Prentice-Hall, Inc., 1970. Examines the compatibility of explanations of behavior as given in psychology or physiology with explanations of the same behavior in terms of wants and beliefs.

LOUCH, A. R., *Explanation and Human Action*. Berkeley and Los Angeles: University of California Press, 1969.

SALMON, WESLEY C., *Statistical Explanation and Statistical Relevance*. Pittsburgh: University of Pittsburgh Press, 1971. A conception of explanation as nondeterministic.

CHAPTER 6   AUTONOMY AND RESPONSIBILITY

AUDI, ROBERT, "Moral Responsibility, Freedom, and Compulsion," *American Philosophical Quarterly*, 11 (1974), 1–14.

AYER, A.J., "Freedom and Necessity," in his *Philosophical Essays*. London: Macmillan and Company, Ltd., 1954. Defends compatibilism.

BEARDSLEY, ELIZABETH L., "A Plea for Deserts," *American Philosophical Quarterly*, 6 (1969), 33–42.

BEROFSKY, BERNARD, ed., *Free Will and Determinism*. New York: Harper and Row, Publishers, 1966. The best collection of articles presenting the standard positions on free will issues.

DUGGAN, TIMOTHY, and BERNARD GERT, "Voluntary Abilities," *American Philosophical Quarterly*, 4 (1967), 127–35; reprinted with slight revisions in Myles Brand, ed., *The Nature of Human Action*. Glenview, Ill.: Scott, Foresman and Company, 1970. An important and useful discussion.

FRANKLIN, R. L., *Freewill and Determinism*. London: Routledge and Kegan Paul, 1968. Defends libertarianism.

FURLEY, DAVID J., "Aristotle and Epicurus on Voluntary Action," in his *Two Studies in the Greek Atomists*. Princeton: Princeton University Press, 1967. Presents an interpretation of the attraction of indeterminism for Epicureans different from the one presented in this book.

HOOK, SIDNEY, ed., *Determinism and Freedom in the Age of Modern Science*. New York: New York University Press, 1961. Most positions are represented in this collection of brief symposium papers and responses.

HOSPERS, JOHN, "Free Will and Psychoanalysis," in *Reason and Responsibility* (3rd ed.), ed. Joel Feinberg. Encino, Calif.: Dickenson Publishing Co., Inc., 1975. Argues for hard determinism.

JAMES, WILLIAM, "The Dilemma of Determinism," in his *Essays in Pragmatism*, ed. Alburey Castell. New York: Hafner Publishing Company, 1966. Argues that indeterminism is more attractive than the alternative.

MORGENBESSER, SIDNEY, and JAMES WALSH, eds., *Free Will*. Englewood Cliffs, N.J.: Prentice-Hall, Inc., 1962. Selections mostly from older writers, including Augustine, Hobbes, and Mill.

NOZICK, ROBERT, "Coercion," in *Philosophy, Science, and Method: Essays in Honor of Ernest Nagel*, ed. S. Morgenbesser, P. Suppes, and M. White, New York: St. Martin's Press, 1969.

OPPENHEIM, FELIX E., *Dimensions of Freedom*. New York: St. Martin's Press, 1961. Deals mostly with political freedom, control of one person by another, etc.

PENNOCK, J. ROLAND, and JOHN W. CHAPMAN, eds., *Coercion: Nomos XIV*. Chicago: Aldine-Atherton, 1972.

INDEX